The Hidden Handshake

The Hidden Handshake

National Identity and Europe in the Post-Communist World

ALEŠ DEBELJAK

Translated by Aleš Debeljak and Rawley Grau

ROWMAN & LITTLEFIELD PUBLISHERS, INC.
Lanham • Boulder • New York • Toronto • Oxford

ROWMAN & LITTLEFIELD PUBLISHERS, INC.

Published in the United States of America
by Rowman & Littlefield Publishers, Inc.
A wholly owned subsidary of The Rowman & Littlefield Publishing Group, Inc.
4501 Forbes Boulevard, Suite 200, Lanham, MD 20706
www.rowmanlittlefield.com

P.O. Box 317, Oxford OX2 9RU, UK

British Library Cataloguing in Publication Information Available

Library of Congress Cataloging-in-Publication Data

Debeljak, Aleš, 1961–
    The hidden handshake : national identity and Europe in the post-communist world /
Aleš Debeljak.
        p. cm.
    Parts of this book have been published as stand-alone essays in an earlier form in
World Literature Today (University of Oklahoma, Norman), East European Politics and
Societies (American Council of Learned Societies), International Journal of Politics,
Culture and Society (Kluwer Academic/Human Sciences Press), and Alternatives (Lynne
Rienner Publishers).
    Includes bibliographical references and index.
    ISBN 0-7425-1779-9 (cloth : alk. paper) — ISBN 0-7425-1780-2 (pbk. : alk. paper)
    1. Political culture—Slovenia. 2. Political culture—Europe. 3. Group identity—
Political aspects—Slovenia. 4. Group identity—Political aspects—Europe. 5. European
federation. 6. Citizenship—Europe. I. Title.
JN2201.A91D4   2004
306.2'094—dc22
                                                                    2004005121
Printed in the United States of America

For Lukas, Simon, Klara, and Erica,
whose love is the best handshake of solidarity I ever received

Contents

Introduction   ix

Chapter 1: National Identity and Citizenship under the
Yoke of Globalization   1

Chapter 2: Slovenia's Absence on the American Cultural Map   25

Chapter 3: The Cosmopolitan Spirit under Siege   59

Chapter 4: Europe without Europeans   93

References   111

Index   115

About the Author   123

Introduction

The following four essays represent an attempt to shed light on forms of thinking that emphasize the dialectic of the self and the larger community. Relying selectively on a social-literary analysis along the lines of the Frankfurt School and, no less importantly, on personal experience as the starting point for my critical meditations, I toyed with the notion that there is value in pursuing a mode of existence that allows one to transcend the parochial limitations of one's national cultural tradition. But cosmopolitan habits can never be completely divorced from an individual's particular cultural background, even if they make it possible to plunge into a whirlwind of diverse linguistic traditions. I was determined, then, to resist the alluring delusions of "free-floating" internationalism, which assumes that a person may be fully at home in a transnational social class and calls for the renunciation of immediate ethnic and cultural ties (for instance, in the name of communist loyalty). While exploring some of the artistic visions that emerged in Slovenia and, more generally, in Central Europe in the twentieth century, I have tried to show that it is possible to remain faithful to the primordial realms of intimate geography, history, and community even as one fosters links to global cultural movements. Defying both the rigidity of nationalist exclusivism and the blithe nonsense of "global citizenship," I have attempted to trace the concentric circles of identity that emanate from images of the self embedded in communal experience and ripple through the currents of national, regional, European, and Atlantic cultures.

Oscillating between longing and memory, these essays try to tease a meaningful message out of the burning bush whose glow illuminates the ruins of the *fin de millénaire* and, therefore, often reach beyond the boundaries of the former Yugoslavia. But unabashedly, my writing springs from the various traditions that animate the troubled region I come from. There is no sense in denying the shock and sorrow I feel in the face of the wanton destruction that Yugoslavia—the country of my birth—suffered at the hands of "national-communist" zealots. Indeed, it may have been the very loss of the multicultural and multireligious mosaic that was Yugoslavia that compelled me to contemplate with such urgency the sediments of the layered identity I once accepted without question: as a Slovene, a Yugoslav, a Central European, and a European. To put it another way, I could see that my ethnic heritage, civic sense, ethical choices, and political predilections had conspired to construct my identity right on top of the fault lines of the immense tectonic shifts that were happening in post–Cold War Europe. In this regard, I began to appreciate the relevance of the democratic order and its institutions, which are, alas, still very much bound to the clearly delineated territory of the nation-state. Despite the havoc perpetrated in the name of nationalism, it would be dangerous to pretend that democratic institutions, even in the contemporary world, have no territorial basis. The spatial solidarity of the territorially defined community may very well be disappearing; in its place, temporary interest groups emerge whose capacity for transterritorial action is crippled, just as their potential for reasonable and consistently moral action is compromised, by their extensive yet loose networks of single-issue agendas. Seen from this perspective, the modern nation-state is not unlike the automobile, the use of which would not be banned outright just because some irresponsible minor on a furtive evening joy ride crashed a car into a tree.

Unlike the strategic planning and geopolitical analysis that goes on at think tanks—which must take into consideration limited possibilities of change "on the ground" as well as the public consequences of the policy proposals they put forth—critical essays are a kind of intellectual poetry, not bound to any imperative of topicality. But this does not mean they are free to wallow in some decontextualized vacuum. My essays are topical not whenever they can be, but only when they must be, in order to maintain the dignity of individual freedom and the necessity of collective life—reaching into a lyric of personal longing while at the same time descending into reservoirs of historical pessimism.

I should also confess something else along these lines. I do not believe that an intellectual, artistic, or cultural critique of the current state of affairs is obliged to bear immediate fruit of the kind that can be measured and managed, as one can do with alterations on a map or the administrative mechanisms of government. It is enough that the right to speak presupposes a belief in the osmotic diffusion of idiosyncratic ideas, perspectives, and visions throughout the layers of the collective mentality. I am not prepared to give up the absurd hope that the global cultural equilibrium shifts ever so slightly whenever some reader sitting alone in her living room decides to keep her eyes fixed on the pages of a small literary magazine rather than gaze at a television screen. For in making this choice, she follows a writer on a journey at the end of which there might await a new perspective, one that would enlarge her field of reality, heighten her sensibility, and fill her nostrils with the strong scent of a place she has certainly never physically entered but that, once having read it, she recognizes as her own.

Immediate biographical reasons, I suppose, dictate my heightened interest in the cross-fertilization of collective and individual existence and lead me to seek the hidden handshake of solidarity. I live in a bilingual and bicultural family. A unique personality is composed of the universal tension between individual loneliness and the public conversation of community. From all the books I read and all the faces I encounter, from a tender hand on my shoulder and from the intellectual passions I pursue throughout the republic of letters, my biography expands and grows. Small wonder, then, that this book of essays is dedicated not only to my American wife but also to my three children, who, in fact, live on a bridge between two cultures, Slovene and American. They have broadened or, rather, sharpened my awareness of the hesitant presence of imagination that gives shape to the narrative of double identity. Conceptual collisions, irritating misunderstandings, and, to be sure, joyful surprises occur almost every day as we speak English in our family, living in the "foreign home" that is our bilingual micro-environment in Ljubljana.

In the vibrations of memory from a childhood spent on the streets of this very town, today the capital of the sovereign Republic of Slovenia, there echo verses from a children's poem by Oton Župančič about a kite: "If you let me go a little higher, / The houses of Trieste I will admire." I, too, flew a kite as a child, but the one in this poem is made of something more than paper and balsa wood. In a metaphorical sense, it outlined the totality of my childhood horizon. I lived with my parents and younger sister in a cluster of low-rise socialist apartment buildings next to the Ljubljanica River, drab façades never quite catching their reflection on the surface of the river's slow-flowing waters. I would gaze through the gently swaying branches of the weeping willows that stood along the riverbank—they have since been removed, perhaps because the architect Jože Plečnik, whose work still defines much of the city's central district, intended them to stand as a visual allusion to bending washerwomen, an emblem of a past now irretrievably lost. Playing on these riverbanks, I tried to imagine invisible worlds in which genuinely dramatic adventures took place that would be worthy of my confused longings. But all I really saw was the northernmost Italian port of Trieste and a faint promise of infinity. It is true that, already as a child, I had a limited stock of concepts shaped by the meager financial means of my parents, the imaginary "other" of the Western capitalist world, and the restrictions of communist Yugoslavia, of which Slovenia was a part. Because of such restrictions, even a short trip to nearby Trieste meant literally entering a different universe. But these are not the kind of limitations I have in mind, although I do not deny the force of prejudice they carry. What I am thinking of is my openness to the evanescent, ever so fragile memories anchored in childhood and permeated with primordial images. Who would not want to understand them? Artistic vision often feeds on the golden era of childhood, because the symbolic archetypes formed at that time govern any meaningful perception of the present. I try not to miss any opportunity to observe this process at work:

how these archetypes confront the use of time and the orientation of space in the present. Such opportunities will arise, especially when playing with and caring for children.

I have three: for all of them, the Slovene language of their father and their mother's American English are equal, though which language they use depends on the immediate suitability of the vocabulary and the flexibility of their descriptions. And so they run through our backyard flying Župančič's kite to the refrains of the English ditty "London Bridge Is Falling Down" and the American round "The Itsy Bitsy Spider," using different tunes to achieve the same goal: to help the sun dry the spidery webs that stretch across other roofs and toward other bridges. My children's horizons reach inevitably much farther than the houses of Trieste. They are spontaneously multiplied, with expanded potential for biography and desire; for my children, the cultural topography of the world is far vaster than it is for me, who grew up in a family entirely Slovene. I am convinced that the sight of fecund surroundings and the feeling of boundless power in the eternal return of the sun are but pillars supporting the frail architecture of the soul. Just as the soul needs landscapes of freedom in order to prepare itself carefully for the certainty of pain and the possible grace of understanding, so, too, the double identity reaches in many directions, hastily opening doors to unknown rooms, seeking new spaces because, extraterritorial as it is, its connection to a single dimension is fading.

The fading of the single tradition is a profound challenge, though it is, perhaps, a uniquely rewarding one. For it points beyond the fundamentalist fear that has, from the very beginnings of Western civilization, enwrapped the "man of a single book" and, analogously, of a single tradition. While the modest aspiration of these essays to inform and enlighten may be, in the eyes of the American reader, somewhat daunted by a large terrain of little-known references to the Central European and Slovene traditions discussed, these essays nonetheless are intended as building blocks for a bridge between cultures.

This book has its roots in a collection of three essays, initially published in Slovene as *Individualism and Literary Metaphors of Nationality* [Individualizem in literarne metafore naroda] (Maribor: Obzorja, 1998). It underwent a number of minor revisions when it was subsequently prepared for publication in Czech, Slovak, Polish, and Hungarian. When preparing the essays for American publication, however, I heavily rewrote most sections, introducing a considerable number of new thoughts, particularly in light of the need to address the current process of European integration and the attendant contradictions that characterize this unprecedented, grand experiment we call the European Union. Neither an enlarged nation-state nor the provisional alliance of independent countries, the European Union represents an astonishing hybrid. Hybridity can be fatiguing inasmuch as it does not correspond to preconceived notions of behavior and thought. But it can be liberating, too, since its malleable features retain a potential for something new, however disfigured it may appear at first glance. In this regard, it seems fitting that this book is neither fully a work of academic scholarship nor fully a work of creative nonfiction, though it makes use of theoretical concepts and is not averse to the poetic impulse behind the personal anecdote.

While this book is, in part, a translation of previously published essays, there is a good deal of newly written material as well, compelled by the theorist's desire to explain and the ethnographer's obligation to inform. For the general educated reader—this figment of many a writer's imagination—the book's focus on details may seem overwhelming, despite the leavening of personal reminiscence intended to mitigate the heavy-duty pressure of ideas. The specialist, on the other hand, might take issue with the occasional generalizations or nutshell accounts of the various intellectual debates that unfold on both sides of the Atlantic. Still, I could not go against my basic instincts, which guided this book toward a consideration of the notion of citizenship, a notion that in modern democratic societies trumps ethnic loyalties; or toward melancholy reveries about the commodified world and aestheticism as window-dressing for horrible realities; or toward contemplation of the archetype of the city as the first nest of humanity, seeking the conditions for a balance between the liberal open mind and nationally grounded experience—as Yael Tamir attempts to do in her admirable *Liberal Nationalism* (Princeton, N.J., 1993). Just as my own mental makeup betrays hybrid features, so, too, does my writing style. From Slovene to American, from Central European to global, my continual reflection on the milestones of my identity must finally yield to a certain epistemological attitude, an intuition about life's profound, sometimes tragic unknowability.

This book, then, does not offer any set of ready-made answers. Rather, it considers its necessary task to be the posing of painful questions. If, in an age of goal-oriented performance, the necessity of contemplation seems a luxury, I have been able to afford it largely thanks to the great patience and encouragement of Dean Birkenkamp, my editor at Rowman & Littlefield. In addition, I am very grateful for the hospitable isolation provided by an artist fellowship at the Renaissance castle of the Civitella Ranieri Center in Umbria, Italy. Similarly, Ilija Tomanić's research assistance, Jana Strgar's and, in particular, Rawley Grau's translation and editorial expertise were indispensable. Although my Slovene and American colleagues were very helpful in my critical pursuit, I alone am responsible for the hope that drives these essays. This hope finds its old-fashioned expression in the belief that Max Müller's famous dictum regarding the individual's understanding of religion can be applied equally well to culture in general: He who knows one, knows none.

The Civitella Ranieri Center
September 2002

Chapter 1

National Identity and Citizenship under the Yoke of Globalization

The Tenuous Bonds of the Nation-State

The last years of the twentieth century were marked by many "ends." Francis Fukuyama promoted "the end of history," Jean Baudrillard discussed "the end of the social," Daniel Bell talked about "the end of ideology," and Michel Foucault analyzed "the end of the subject." But if anything, the end of the twentieth century bore witness, I suspect, to the end of the modern nation-state.

The modern nation-state grew out of the emancipatory movements of nineteenth-century Europe. The intellectual elites of a number of subjugated ethnic groups rebelled against the multinational Russian and Austrian empires and joined forces with fledgling entrepreneurs in a call for collective autonomy. The political advantages of the independent nation-state over a monarchical structure have qualified these nineteenth-century national movements as progressive and liberal. Forged from numerous principalities and fiefdoms that were once mutually hostile, the nation-state evolved around a chosen ethnic nucleus. The language of this nucleus served as a rallying point for groups from neighboring regions to coalesce into a larger, more abstract whole. Modern industrial society, in which the idea of the nation-state was firmly embedded, required as a rule a standardized language that could facilitate the management of a multiethnic and multilingual labor force. The dialect of the most economically developed region was often elevated to the level of a linguistic standard to which all the other similar vernacular idioms had to adhere. The political idea of the nation-state as a unifying force thus drew sustenance from cultural sources, which, in turn, supplied the public with the material for narratives of self-identification, as Rudi Rizman suggests in his essay "The Relevance of Nationalism for Democratic

Citizenship." Although divided by social class, education, and sometimes even religion, the diverse segments of a population could look to a common bond, which the intellectual elite had patched up from scraps of folklore and myth.

For two hundred years, the nation-state was the supreme provider of collective meaning; not even such alternative international movements as communism, which located solidarity in social class rather than ethnic identity, could seriously undermine its position. Right up to World War II, the nation-state thus more or less successfully controlled all forces and tendencies, including economic ones, throughout its territory. But today, such control is next to impossible. Multinational corporations increasingly focus their efforts on developing global markets—beyond any specific political, linguistic, or ethnic borders—where companies prosper by offering products with ingredients and images that are the same everywhere, such as Levi's jeans, Coca-Cola, or Microsoft Word for Windows. In the process, these corporations tacitly spell out the rules for the operation of individual nation-state governments. "National" sources of capital, then, are not only difficult to identify but also increasingly irrelevant.

It would appear that culture, with its habits of the heart and its symbolic behavior, its visual representations and its linguistic idiosyncrasies, may represent the last remaining sphere of human activity able to preserve some features of the specific collective life, which, insofar as I am concerned here, is the national experience. At the risk of taking the part for the whole, I would like to draw on the example of Slovenia as a basis for the consideration of certain long-term social processes that might suggest a potential truce between the particular national tradition and the universal mechanisms of globalization. In this regard, the Slovene experience should be seen as an illustration of broader mental structures that may be applicable, with a certain degree of heuristic caution, to other numerically small Central European nations. What interests me is, I confess, something fairly abstract. The vicissitudes of a political community, where solidarity depends not only on a shared life-world and the spontaneity of love, but also on strenuous reflection and critical consideration, always resist unambiguous interpretation. Yet one thing, at least, seems clear to me: it is impossible to live sensibly without some sort of anchorage in the collective, although it is certainly possible to die senselessly in its name. While I hope I am courageous enough to refuse a senseless death, I nonetheless believe that collective forms of existence are not, by design, stifling; nor are they only stifling. They may provide palpable feelings of belonging that are as hard to dismiss as the bonds of tradition are difficult to break.

A personal recollection might serve to illustrate my point. In June 2001, Slovenia celebrated the tenth anniversary of its independence and its establishment as a sovereign nation-state. This was a unique event in the history of the Slovene people, who, after a long tradition of limited autonomy, had acquired full national sovereignty only in 1991, following a Ten Day War with the Yugoslav Army. To mark the occasion, the country's leading statesmen assembled for an official ceremony on Republic Square in Ljubljana. We ordinary people commemorated our independence each in his or her own way. I watched the firework display over Ljubljana Castle from a distance, leaning on the garden fence in front of my house—I was observing the public sphere from across the threshold of privacy, as it were. And I was not alone; many of my neighbors, too, gazed over the tops of the old acacia trees that grew in the schoolyard across the street. We had all trickled out of our suburban houses that evening to watch the colorful traceries of light, which, besides providing visual delight, were supposed to remind us that an event of great importance was taking place.

I live on Zvezna Ulica—Union Street—originally a reference to the now disintegrated Yugoslav federation. As the summer days grew warmer, the truth of this history welled up in my mind, as I listened to the "ethnic mix" of Croatian, Bosnian, Slovene, and Roma dialects—a hodge-podge that went far beyond standard Slovene—which the gang of kids gathering under the corner street lamp had devised for communication among themselves as they went about their lively business (which, in the eyes of our traditional working-class neighborhood, often meant they were "up to no good"). Nearly every night that summer, when I went out into the yard to smoke one last cigarette before bed, I would observe these kids as, under a murky circle of lamplight, they tried out various styles of power, authority, and compromise, vying for group leadership. But for me, the name of my street recalls something more than the union that once brought these kids' parents together in a single political state; I prefer to imagine that it hints at one of the most crucial determinants of the human condition, a much broader kind of association and community, flirting with connotations from a different stock of meaning and opening spaces for the continuity of a shared life. The hidden handshake of solidarity implied in the name of my street urges me to reflect on something that is existentially relevant for individual identity, and, indeed, for collective identity, too: not only tolerance, but the possibility of understanding and respect for "the other."

The Slovene writer Marjan Rožanc (1930–1990) has movingly depicted such regard for "the other" in his 1979 novel *Love* [Ljubezen], which, coincidentally, is set in my very neighborhood, Zelena Jama. The novel, which was later made into an acclaimed film, is set at the time of the Italian occupation of Ljubljana during World War II and written from the perspective of an adolescent boy. The characters are politically divided between the "Red" communist and "black" Roman Catholic groups. The war has sharpened the conflict between the two factions to bloody extremes. What redeems things is, ultimately, love—a fragile, innocent love, based on the authority of a child's direct and unquestioning acceptance. Love, for Rožanc, is an ecumenical force. Its ability to serve as the basic glue of solidarity derives, surely, from the fact that it functions transpolitically. Rožanc's young narrator loves the communist activists with the same disarming passion he bestows on the youths that collaborated with the Fascists and Nazis, since what excites, inspires, and delights him most is the whole of the neighbourhood community, complete with its internal quarrels, conflicts, and disputes. If the novel teaches us anything, it is the imperative to seek and cherish the things that bind a community together, whether the community is something immediate and concrete, like the Zelena Jama neighborhood, or something rather distant and abstract, like the Slovene nation-state or, even more so, the European federation as it strives to emerge from the current struggles within European Union. But admittedly, the microcosm of a neighborhood is much easier to imagine, especially since Rožanc's literary masterpiece endows the love and solidarity among its inhabitants with such vivid, emotionally charged forms—forms that continue, in more than one way, to mold the local community even today.

Is Patriotism Obsolete?

Abstract though it may be, the Slovene nation-state, ten years after gaining its independence—and making its escape—from communist Yugoslavia, is now confronted with the central question of its collective existence: entry into a new association, a new federation, a new unity—the European Union. But here I must note certain reservations. First of all, there is the subordinate status that the post-communist candidate nations have been compelled to accept during the E.U. expansion process. I am suspicious, too, about the European Union's often-criticized "democratic deficit," which is apparent, at the very least, in the fact that the European Commission, its primary decision-making body, is led by appointed, not elected politicians. Then, there is Europe's underdeveloped public sphere, hampered by a lack of media and forums for genuine transnational debate, not only among politicians, but also among nongovernmental organizations and, especially, citizens themselves.

Greater moral and political solidarity across national borders would be another important integrating factor in developing new forms of belonging together and a heightened awareness of interconnectedness. In this regard, the European Union's shameful passivity in the wars of the Yugoslav secession can hardly be considered accidental. Rather, it was an unmistakable sign of distrust of Europe's *terra incognita*—the Balkans, that dark subcontinent within the continent. To put it in the trivializing prose of Western Europe's everyday perceptions: Bosnians, Croats, Kosovar Albanians, and the other victims of Serb national socialism were not seen as genuine, full-blooded Europeans and so were hardly worth the investment in any organized effort to stop the attempted genocide until things had gotten well out of hand.

Considering all this, the Slovene people cannot easily accept the annulment of an essential part of their sovereignty or lightly ponder the consequences of handing it over to a transnational entity such as the European Union. This is no simple matter, especially in post-communist states where national sovereignty has only recently been won. Slovenia—unlike Hungary, Lithuania, or Poland—has never in all its history existed as a separate and independent nation. While Western European intellectuals and (to a lesser extent) politicians were discussing the gradual decline of the nation-state within the context of globalization—as they had been doing at least since the 1960s—Slovenes, in fact, hopped on the last car of the last train of nationalism as a legitimate movement toward national statehood. It is thus no accident that Slovenes, like other Central Europeans, still see ourselves predominantly as members of an ethnically based state, while most West European countries, not to mention the United States, have already begun to see themselves largely as multicultural and multireligious communities in which the main principle of public life is no longer one's ethnic membership but, rather, respect for the law and the constitution. The practice of a common way of life, then, is no longer considered to be entirely dependent on ethnic identity but, instead, is more closely linked to the ideal of *constitutional patriotism,* as Jürgen Habermas would have it, following Dolf Sternberger's studied rejection, in the early 1980s, of the national.

Ethnic identity, however, is far from obsolete and is certainly more accessible than the tangled political deliberation that informs constitutional patriotism: unlike other foundations for human unity, ethnic identity has a dubious advantage in that it naturalizes history. That is to say, it regards culture as a natural phenomenon and freedom as a necessary given. The nation-state, which promotes the principle of ethnic unity at the expense of all other loyalties, is the only story of successful community in the modern age, as Zygmunt Bauman argues in his recent book, *Liquid Modernity* (New York, 2000). Nationalism is the only ideology that has carried out its often violent ambitions for general community status with a considerable measure of conviction and effectiveness. The Romantic ideal of a single people with a single language that embodies the nation's unique, untranslatable, and inalienable spirit has been particularly successful in Central and Eastern Europe. Here the philosophy of nationhood as something organic, as Herder interpreted it, found a much more fertile ground than did the idea of a universal civic identity such as was emphasized in the French Revolution and the Enlightenment. The idea that the unity and self-respect of a particular people could be legitimately based on ethnic identity did, of course, receive an important boost from German Romanticism. But we need to remember, too, that the success of the nation-state was due to the fact that it was able to control the economic, social, educational, and cultural resources on its territory. It managed to suppress or even crush all other groups struggling to assert themselves. It aggressively undermined provincial authorities and local ways of life, imposing a single standard language and a single historical memory and pushing to the side other traditions, whether regional or linguistic, such as the Provençal, Corsican, and Breton languages in France or the Friulian and Sicilian dialects in Italy.

If we agree that even today it is relatively difficult to think outside the frame of the nation-state or, more precisely, of ethnic tradition—which, no matter how we try, we cannot simply discard like a worn-out dress—it would be wise, I think, to consider the difference between patriotism and nationalism. Without splitting academic hairs, one can say that patriotism is a nationalism that has been tamed and civilized; it can even be something noble. George Orwell, in his classic essay "Politics and the English Language" (1946), described patriotism as a repudiation of the most undesirable, shameful, and brutal aspects of nationalist chauvinism. A nationalist who believes in his nation as the incar-

nation of the Supreme Ideal, a mystical Truth, will do anything he can to ensure
the collective existence of those like himself. He will even resort violence and
xenophobia so as to indulge more easily in the illusion that the blunders and
failings of his own nation are entirely the fault of some foreign conspiracy.

The patriot, in contrast, is a citizen whose behavior in a democratic political
order is guided by a tolerance for cultural diversity and, especially, for ethnic
and religious minorities. The patriot considers it self-evident that these minorities should enjoy legal guarantees that allow them to celebrate their own traditions, just as he himself is not ashamed of his own membership in an ethnic
collective or squeamish about the emotional charge that comes with it. Karl
Schurtz, a nineteenth-century German revolutionary who emigrated to the
United States, fought in the American Civil War, and later became an important
statesman, famously proclaimed his allegiance to his adopted land by declaring,
"My country, right or wrong!" On the face of it, this seems the quintessentially
nationalistic sentiment. Yet, Schurtz's next sentence, which is often conveniently overlooked in public discussion, sets the record straight: "When right to
be kept right, when wrong, to be put right." These two sentiments taken together—allegiance to one's nation along with a critical attitude toward such
membership—form the backbone of *intelligent* patriotism. As Robert McClure
suggests, this kind of patriotism is never arrogant, while crude nationalism always is.

A Common Mental Landscape

In the room in which I gather these words there stands a modest Biedermeier
chest of drawers. It first caught my wife's eye on one of our frequent autumn
walks through the streets of Old Ljubljana, soon after our return from America
in the early 1990s. It was standing in the shop window of an antique store at 17
Town Square, a bourgeois mansion with a pastel-colored neoclassicist façade.
Whenever I look at this chest of drawers, its polished curves remind me of the
bitter pang I felt that day, as I realized that the boundaries of my language were,
to a considerable degree, the boundaries of my world, too. I am not talking
merely about the extent of my linguistic skills. I am speaking, rather, of the
whole symbolic, mental, and social experience deposited in the layers of a nation's historical existence and collective mentality. Individuals absorb the collective mentality through language, which is not merely some mechanical means
of communication but, first and foremost, the encapsulation of a metaphysical
worldview. And this worldview was not something I could ever fully convey to
my wife, a New Yorker who was born in California.

Erica viewed the mansion with the eyes of an interested foreigner who had
over time developed a deep affection for Slovenes and Slovenia, her newly
adopted home. In the building's faded charm, she saw only the appeal of simple
proportions, a gentle intimation of the past, and contended pigeons on the win-
dowsill. That, I suspect, is how she views most of the townhouses that flank the

green Ljubljanica River. How difficult it was to explain that my view was both broader and deeper, drawing as it did on the kind of cultural vocabulary every national identity possesses. I had for many years studied first-hand the cultural and social history of my wife's country, yet I am aware that I could not fully appreciate the intricacies of the diverse American heritage.

How difficult it was to explain, then, that this building, the Erberg Mansion (and now, among other things, the home of the Slovenian Film and Theater Museum), inevitably conjured up a string of associations for me: The Baroque painter Fortunatus Bergant died here in 1769. The preeminent Slovene Romantic poet France Prešeren (1800–1849) lived here as a schoolboy, in crowded quarters with his two younger brothers; later, after a yearlong stint as resident tutor for the Pagliaruzzi family at Cekin Palace in Ljubljana's Tivoli Park, the poet returned to live in another house in this same courtyard. In 1914, the year when Archduke Franz Ferdinand, heir to the Habsburg throne, was struck down in Sarajevo by the bullets of Gavrilo Princip, the poet Milan Jarc lived here in a small student's cell on the third floor; it was possibly here that he conceived the first poems for *Man and the Night* [Človek in noč] (1927), a book permeated with the restless sorrow of a war-shaken soul and vague expressionist inspiration. How could I tell my wife, in no uncertain terms, that all these associations concerned something more than just artists and writers? Well, all right, perhaps that could be done. So let me rephrase my predicament: If you paid close enough attention, you might indeed manage to grasp the basic significance of the names that flickered through my erratic cultural memory as if on a worn-out strip of film. But this sprawling array of literary tidbits and visual details, this rich catalog of historical images evoked by the Erberg Mansion, where the hallways still echo with the fleeting footsteps of these artists—this mental landscape is simply too vast to be adequately summarized. Yet most reasonably schooled Slovenes have absorbed such things from their textbooks and general education.

This historical arch spans the Baroque colorism of Bergant's portrait of Joseph Anton Codelli—where the painter's characteristic signature is cleverly written along the edge of the table on which the smug burgher leans—as well as the impulsive raggedness of Jarc and Prešeren's refined lyricism with its "trace of shadow from the dawn of otherworldly glory"—a poetic description of unattainable transcendence, which, alas, cannot be translated into English without the risk of making Prešeren sound like some stilted Byronic derivative. Prešeren's work has, in fact, been translated in several editions (most recently in 2001), but these were all published only in Slovenia—an accurate, if sad, indication of the boundaries within which Prešeren speaks to Slovenes and to hardly anyone else.

In this spontaneous swirl of images that shape my imaginative horizon, the distinguishing features of the national cultural heritage are revealed. This heritage binds me, in its existential dimension, more fatefully than the cultures of the "global village" I pretend to know or of the shattered Yugoslav mosaic, my "native realm." It provides me with a framework for recognizing my hopes and sorrows—things, I believe, that can be expressed authentically only in a language that takes sustenance from one's primary socialization, the internalized pictures of a world in which nothing is without a name. This is but another way of talking about a home, the absolute reality of a place in which images and ideas, allusions and metaphors are, more likely than not, grasped without reflection, as "second nature."

The Necessity of the Collective Narrative

Just think for a moment of King Arthur and the Knights of the Round Table; the *Nibelungenlied;* the long campaign of Russia's Prince Igor; the royal bones that molder in the crypt of Krakow's Wawel Castle and dully animate the Polish imagination whenever the calendar of national rituals requires a public performance. Most European nations are able to find, in the palimpsests of their collective past, metaphysical meaning in some narrative about their history—something that in moments of crisis lends support to their worldly endeavors, cultural pride, and group identity. History, as is well known, means a story or narrative. Evidence of this can be found in the linguistic precision of the English word itself: *hi-story.* "Story" helps shape the space of "history" from the inside. There is, indeed, nothing surprising in the fact that the significance of an individual biography, the story of a man or woman, can reach full expression only within the framework of a particular collective tradition. The story of this tradition brings meaningful order to a seething chaos of facts. Facts become facts only in the light of theory, that is, in weaving raw data into a coherent story. We have access to the hopes and fears, whether of the individual or the collective, only through the form of a narrative. In public encounters between its multiple versions, a flowing narrative about the past emerges, responding to and accommodating a community's current sense of itself. The way you look over your shoulder determines the way you look at the present.

But there are two kinds of narrative: the story of history and the vision of art. Art is always a narrative about something concrete and, in this way, is even truer than history, which is a narrative about something general, as Aristotle's *Poetics* tells us, and there is no reason to doubt this ancient truth. I would much rather, then, devote myself to poems and novels than to the value-free discourse of political economy or the topsy-turvy rhetoric of televised talking heads, if only to seek that special grace in which "life is enriched most by that narrative which is faithful to the complexity of history, which opens the greatest space for human creativity and, through the elegance of its form, attains a certain kind of transcendence and speaks to the best aspect of our being," as Neil Postman put it in his plenary speech at the 1993 Frankfurt Book Fair.

And what of the Slovenes? Slovenes find the gentle murmur of inspiration not only in the positivism of cultural history but also, and perhaps more strongly, in "national mythology"—even if it is held together by a modest roster of such figures as Beautiful Vida, a wet nurse to the Spanish royal family who tearfully pines for her homeland; Črtomir, a pagan warlord, defeated by encroaching Christians; Peter Klepec, a weakling shepherd turned superhero; King Mathias, who waits with his soldiers in the heart of a mountain, ready to liberate the Slovene lands; Martin Krpan, a triumphant peasant who defends the royal Viennese court against the Turks; and, last but not least, Jernej the hireling, a rebellious proletarian, and Martin Čedermac, an anti-Fascist Catholic preacher. These figures entered the public imagination straight out of Slovene folklore and early modern literature.

But their symbolic meaning is far from fixed as competing public interpretations negotiate the conflict between grand public deeds in the name of a larger group and the private desire for a good life. Specifically, these heroes reveal how the Slovenes' collective dilemma has always been wedded to the problem of a cultural identity that goes unacknowledged by their adversaries—whether Germans and Austrians, under whom the Slovenes lived for eleven long centuries, or Serbs, with whom, and often under whom, the Slovenes lived for seventy years in the "common Yugoslav house." The heroes of the Slovene national mythology first had to carve out an identity for themselves and then had to take pains to make it publicly recognized. In Slovene culture—and especially in literature as the paramount modern substitute for mythology—this fundamental archetype of the "rites of passage" can be seen to occur over and over again. This archetype echoes with allusions that make it relevant even for modern-day Slovenes, though I admit that today's collective inspiration may be drawn more from the international icons of the culture industries than from locally published novels. Still, I would suggest that these traditional figures are perhaps especially needed today, now that Slovenes are living in an independent nation-state. It may seem paradoxical, but it is hardly incorrect to say that the long-term political vision regarding this state focuses solely on its potential for economic success and all too easily forgets that it was established primarily for the purpose of protecting national interests. In other words, Slovenes created the independent nation-state in order truly *to be,* and not only superficially *to have*—if I might paraphrase one of Erich Fromm's classic conceptual pairings.

Metaphorically speaking, the Slovene nation-state exists so that the Slovene language, together with the culture it expresses as the basic structure of thought and emotion, can be exercised in ways that go far beyond the condescending use to which the Austrian emperors put Slovene. They used it to communicate with their horses. The leading Slovene poet of the twentieth century, the prophetic Edvard Kocbek (1904–1981), fashioned this pregnant metaphor in his poem "The Lippizaners" [Lipicanci] written in the 1960s:

Others have worshiped holy cows and dragons,
thousand-year-old turtles and winged lions,
unicorns, double-headed eagles and phoenixes,
but we've chosen the most beautiful animal,
which proved to be excellent on battlefields, in circuses,
harnessed to princesses and the Golden Monstrance,
therefore the emperors of Vienna spoke
French with skillful diplomats,

Italian with charming actresses,
Spanish with the infinite God,
and German with uneducated servants:
but with the horses they talked Slovene.

(Translated by Sonja Kravanja)

Slovene, then, is something more than just an instrument of technical-formal communication; it is more than just a language one happens to speak. When its public use is neglected, disdained, or infringed upon, the unique truth of the collective mentality gradually deteriorates. As Theodor W. Adorno observed, what is poorly expressed is also poorly thought. It would seem likely, then, that you can "think well," that is, with the totality of your being, only in the language that allows you to express yourself intimately, with a vocabulary of love, prayer, and poetry in which an almost physical urge overrides critical reflection. In this sense, it is not difficult to see the mother tongue as the primary element of cultural identity. If we do not use the mother tongue for all complex forms of discourse (commerce, economics, science, administration, medicine, and so on), which alone can express a complex view of reality, then it will be nothing more than the language of a handicapped nation.

Language as a World View

In Slovene history it was the Romantics who best understood the fateful connection between language and national identity—that is, the image of a nation as a society of the living, the dead, and the yet-to-be-born. France Prešeren (1800–1848), who wrote with equal elegance in Slovene and German, is a case in point. German was the *lingua franca* of Central Europe up until World War I. To reject German as a literary medium, like Prešeren did, meant a divorce from the dominant linguistic sphere, with its large market and stimulating cultural life. But Prešeren's commitment to his mother tongue represented a different set of values. His decision was not simply about a choice of medium, about whether to swap one mode of expression for another in order to gain easier access to certain resources. For him, using Slovene was an article of faith, an existential and political decision that seems especially relevant today. If the mother tongue presents a particular worldview, it also represents a specific comprehensive perspective that cannot be adequately expressed in any other language. For me as a poet, this perspective is of fundamental importance in discussing affairs of culture, its pitfalls and its strengths.

Another anecdote, anyone? Thank you. Exhale, inhale: here I go.

An undergraduate student at the University of Ljubljana once ruefully declared, after one of my lectures, that he really was not sure what made him a Slovene. He surfs the Internet, watches MTV and Hollywood slash-and-burn movies, and shops at Benneton and the Gap; meanwhile, the rural idyll of Slovenian hayracks with its peasant rituals and festivities has about as much meaning for him as sepia photos in a dusty album. All this is quite understandable. In our post-national world, I am sure he is not alone in his predicament: Who am I? Where do I belong? I often wonder about such things, too. Nevertheless, when without warning I switched in the midst of our conversation from Slovene into a rapid, idiomatic English, my student blinked. He suddenly realized that his selectively fed English, despite being the language of international mass culture, uncomfortably limited his expressive register and flattened out his imaginative horizon. For many aspects of the national experience are, I believe, integrated in the unique perspective of the mother tongue and the cultural capital it nurtures.

The haven of mother tongue is, then, the place where every single thing has a name, as I have already noted. Only in its unique perspective are all the cultural, political, geographical, symbolic, and social continuities of the national experience present in a self-evident way. Language, then, transcends us as individuals, for it is older and greater than time, which, in turn, is older and greater than space, as Joseph Brodsky observed in his poetic essay "To Please a Shadow." I hasten to add that I, too, find nationalistic exclusivism, which detests all that is foreign and different, to be most repulsive. But this does not mean that I must, by some default, subscribe to the other extreme, the total rejection of national cultural experience.

I spent a number of years in America; at home in Ljubljana, I speak American English with my wife, who is still learning Slovene. When I write essays and articles (though not poems!) for the foreign press, I write with mild frustration but passable ease in the *lingua Americana*—as today's language of international communication might ironically be called. All the same, I cannot join the chorus of the many Slovene politicians of economic reductionism and parvenus of the post-communist transition who cheerfully proclaim that the renunciation of the mother tongue, five hundred words of elementary-school English, and a cozy familiarity with the universal imagery of cable television automatically brings them "closer to Europe" and, to boot, guarantees them the coveted badge of liberal largesse. This is not because I think it is not cost-efficient to translate every state document and professional contract into a foreign language, or rather, into English. From the strictly economic viewpoint, it doesn't pay to exist as a small independent country in the first place. No, the primary reason I cannot join in this chorus is because I believe that a person of flesh and blood does not live by bread alone.

Make no mistake: I am not advocating the privilege of starvation. On the contrary. But to live without a spiritual realm where both individual and group experience can be fully articulated means to exist in a sad sort of limbo. For this reason, then, the economic success story that every post-communist state yearns for must necessarily be accompanied by a cultural success story. While economic success may be indexed on the stock market, a nation's cultural success story is more elusive, for it encapsulates the symbolic and material aspects of the language, public values, the burden of history, and the limitations of tradition. This cultural story helps us make sense of our lives as part of the larger national life, as a link in the "great chain of being" that will continue long after

we are gone. Today, when global integration and such processes as the enlargement of European Union make the cultures of the smaller nations seem a fussy
inconvenience, steadfast efforts are needed to keep the cultural story going. The
mother tongue and its culture may be the dominant, but are by no means the
only forces that shape individual identity. The stronger the demand for socialization into a "universal" model of behavior, the greater is the human need for
one's own individuality, identity, and anchorage.

Of course, I hear rancorous objections: Why on earth is it still necessary to
preserve national culture and language if, in an independent nation-state, the
complete set of political, economic and social institutions are finally in place?
After all, the whole point of the national movement was to establish such institutions, and now that they exist, the movement has run its course. In a world
dominated by global financial transactions, increasing creolization, and extensive communication technologies, the claim that culture no longer has to be the
primary mark of national identity seems innocuous enough: the management of
the *res publica* can now be left exclusively to professional politicians and the
checks and balances of parliamentary democracy. But it seems to me that even
in an independent state, a broad-based maintenance of cultural consciousness is
essential. And not only because it is something far too important to leave to
politicians. After our long and arduous road as part of Yugoslavia, Slovenes
should not be too quick to sign up as Vienna's stableboys yet again—to use a
metaphor that dramatizes the servile attitude of the Slovenian political elite toward the "paradise lost" of Europe and its grand experiment in regulated national coexistence, the European Union.

The current situation raises new questions about the purpose and meaning
of collective identity. It is particularly relevant for Central and East European
countries whose urban centers today reveal a substantially higher degree of ethnic homogeneity than they did at the beginning of the last century. Throughout
the twentieth century, the cities of Krakow, Prague, Budapest, and Ljubljana—
both as urban spaces and as hubs of their respective national aspirations—underwent not only modernization and industrialization but also a defining and decisive transformation in their collective identities: they made national culture—
that is, one based on a specific chosen ethnic tradition—into their dominant
culture. As a rule, this meant a more or less violent de-Germanization—which at
the very least indicates how extensive and powerful the Austrian empire had
been.

The terrible wars for Yugoslav succession in the 1990s—in which latter-day
Serbian fascists became obsessed with the totalitarian idea that their nation-state
had to expand anywhere a Serbian soldier had ever set foot—helped blot out the
Slovenes' memory of just how suppressed our culture had been before we joined
Yugoslavia, when we were part of the Austro-Hungarian Empire. When the
Kingdom of the Serbs, Croats, and Slovenes—as Yugoslavia was originally
called—came into being in 1918, it was necessary to Slovenize all the high
schools on Slovene ethnic territory within the kingdom. Before World War I and
the fall of Habsburgs, all secondary schools—with the sole exception of the private Roman Catholic Gymnasium in the Ljubljana suburbs—had been steeped

in the German cultural-linguistic tradition. Similarly, before 1918, four of the territory's eight teacher's colleges had been bilingual, while instruction at the other four was conducted entirely in German. It was only as a constituent part of Yugoslavia that Slovenes, for the first time in history, could attend an institution of advanced learning that had Slovene as the language of instruction, namely, the University of Ljubljana, which became chartered with five colleges in the summer of 1919. The same holds true for the national library, the academy of arts and sciences, and so on. In short, before the creation of the first Yugoslavia, the Slovenes essentially had no national economic, educational, or political institutions of their own. These were acquired only within the context of the Yugoslav cohabitation—though not without grumbling from the royal Serbian court in Belgrade. After the defeat of the Axis forces and the end of World War II, the second Yugoslavia emerged. As a federation, its constitutional provisions contained a legal foundation for Slovene statehood as the (albeit) Socialist Republic of Slovenia.

Neither Russians nor Prussians

My point is that, as pleased as the Slovene public is today to share borders with Western Europe and as horrified as it has been by the Serbian military madness in the Balkans, it is wise to keep in mind that the influence of the German-Austrian paradigm on the Slovene mentality has hardly been benevolent. The recent Serbian politics of expansionism was clearly anachronistic in the way it resorted to artillery fire in its effort to convince other Southern Slavic nations of Serb superiority. But this does not mean one should lose sight of the fact that, in a postmodern world, domination no longer expresses itself through armaments. Instead, it sings a seductive song about "ethnically neutral" economics, transnational capital, and homogenizing cultural patterns. If Slovenes want to survive as a distinct nation in a period of rapid global integration, more is needed than just a set of Slovene economic institutions able to participate actively in the international marketplace. The national opera and theater are also of critical importance; not only the efforts of Slovene traders and merchants, but also of a host of public radio and television stations are required; we need not only the successes of Slovene diplomats, but also the achievements of artists and intellectuals. Granted, these cultural endeavors may not reach easily beyond the state borders, but still, they may remind those of us within that the collective Slovene dilemma, at least since independence, no longer has to be summarized by the defeatist dictum of the nineteenth-century writer Fran Levstik: "We will be either Russians or Prussians!" We Slovenes can now be ourselves.

The notion that the Slovenes were culturally, economically, and socially more developed than the other nations in Yugoslavia—both in the kingdom and the Socialist Federation—was rarely challenged publicly in the other Yugoslav republics. But that sense of achievement is of little use today when the primary political context for Slovenia is no longer Yugoslav but European. In other words, the Slovene nation has made the transition from being a big fish in the pond of Yugoslavia to being a little fish in the sea of Europe. We could even say, a tiny fish. But live it must, tiny or not.

A nation with a fully developed cultural identity, of course, has no problem confronting challenges and influences from the outside. In the case of Slovenia, there should be little doubt about the existence of a national cultural identity. The accomplishments of its leading writers, artists, and other creative minds provide the Slovene nation with a strong sense of cultural identity despite having a population of only two million people. But let me emphasize that these creative accomplishments must not be understood as Slovene in an exclusively ethnic sense; there has always existed a vibrant, if small, buzz of creative and intellectual voices that actively contribute to Slovene public life without necessarily being steeped in ethnic Slovene traditions.

It is true that, since gaining independence, Slovenes have had great difficulty adopting a stance of linguistic ecumenism toward citizens of Slovenia who do not speak Slovene. This is primarily because Slovene, as the language of a stateless people, had been in a subordinate position for hundreds of years. So it is not surprising that Slovenes, an endangered nation, tended to view all foreigners with suspicion. As an old Slovene saying goes, the snake of history has so often bitten us that now even a coiled rope can scare us. Nevertheless, there is in Slovenia, especially within artistic circles, a subtle but invaluable tradition of openness toward foreigners who contribute to the development of our culture. The thing that introduces people to the larger world, where their existential experience can be fully acknowledged, is not some misguided notion of the nefarious privileges of "blood and soil" but, rather, an active participation in the mechanisms of cultural creativity. For the sake of argument, let me go further. A foreigner is not someone who was born outside of Slovenia but the one who feels less bound to the Slovene national experience than, let us say, to the almighty logic of profit maximization. Especially in our post–Cold War world, which has witnessed mass migrations of refugees, intellectuals, artists, and entrepreneurs, as well as frenzied transactions of international capital, this profit principle has become so widespread that an extremely appealing illusion has arisen among the professional classes: Never before, it seems, has it been so easy to voluntarily give up one's native language without at the same time experiencing cultural rigor mortis.

This does not mean, however, we should not welcome the creative "draft tunnel"—both the dialogue and the tension that foreigners bring to any country. Quite the contrary. If, in the process of living alongside those who were not born in the same city or national culture, we are forced to examine our lives all the more carefully, then the interaction between foreigners and natives becomes truly productive. Foreign songs, foreign symbols, and foreign languages cannot help but invite us to review the criteria and values we would otherwise take for granted. This sort of "dialogic" mode of life is certainly not simple, but it is politically more democratic, spiritually richer, and existentially more fruitful. A culture or a nation that lives in isolation—even if by choice—inevitably starts to sink into the slime of historical oblivion. First it becomes stiflingly parochial, then belligerently tribal, and finally, it disappears altogether.

The Benefits of Civic Identity

Slovenes, indeed, must be willing to deal with other sorts of mentalities and behaviors so as not to succumb completely to self-sufficiency, parochial xeno-phobia, various forms of exclusivism, and eventual national barrenness. "The other" becomes incomprehensible, robbed of humanity, and thus an enemy, only when members of a given national polity are unsure of their own negotiated identity. My life in different cities and countries—a palpable engagement with "the other"—helped me to see how impossible it was to turn my back on Slove-nia's treasure trove of national cultural references. Such references allowed me to appreciate the particularities of other cultural traditions. I came to realize that a true cosmopolitan is one who can confidently move about the world without forgetting his or her national origins and ethnic background.

Examples are easy to find. Early in his life, James Joyce left Ireland—that sow who devours her own children—without any desire to return, but wherever he lived—Trieste, Pula, or Zurich—he wrote obsessively one and the same story, the story of his darkly beautiful, disgustingly attractive Dublin. Pablo Picasso skillfully mobilized the mysterious virile powers of his Spanish nature on the Left Bank of the Seine, far from his actual "native realm." And it is a fragrant Caribbean universe that emanates from the poems of Derek Walcott, who writes in voluntary exile in the United States. Then there is Rainer Maria Rilke, who once famously exclaimed that "all homelands are empty." Although his mastery of French enabled him to pen a book of poems that delighted even Valéry's discriminating ear, Rilke nevertheless drew on an unmistakably Ger-manic tradition.

The case of Slovenia is not without similar examples of cross-cultural polli-nation. Emyl Korytko, a Polish émigré in nineteenth-century Ljubljana, gathered Slovene folk songs and ethnographic material long before this task was assumed by ethnic Slovene scholars. Maria Nablocka, an admired actress between the two world wars, was a member of defeated "White" Russian community that flooded Europe after the October Revolution. Lily Novy, a prominent early-twentieth-century poet, was one of the pillars of Slovene literary modernism even though her ethnic background was Austrian. Branko Gavella, a Croatian theatre director, was instrumental in expanding the expressive forms of the per-forming arts in Slovenia, while Czech film director František Čap, with a num-ber of hugely popular movies, almost single-handedly established the founda-tions for modern Slovenian film making in the years following World War II. Among contemporary participants in Slovene culture, I could mention Josip Osti, a prolific and much-celebrated Bosnian writer; Jette Ostan, a Danish thea-tre actress; and Svava Bernhardsdottir, an Icelandic violinist with the Slovenian Philharmonic Orchestra.

Such a random sampling serves only as a limited illustration of my principled insistence on separating ethnic and civic identity. Nevertheless, I hope these examples reveal some glimpse of the rich participation of people from foreign lands, however small in number, in Slovenia's cultural life. These people chose their new civic identity without giving up their attachment to the ethnic communities they came from. The notions of civic identity and the concomitant "constitutional patriotism" are, to be sure, far from being fully established as the norm in independent Slovenia; yet such artists as these help outline the possibilities for multiple identities available in a modern secular polity, the chief guarantor of which is the democratic nation-state.

Some Obscure Lessons of History

The separation of ethnic and civic identities is especially important for me, since multiple identities had, up until mid-1970s, considerable public currency in the country of my birth, the former Yugoslav federation. Undemocratic as the country was, an individual citizen, nevertheless, could have at least a dual identity, as an ethnic Croat, Slovene, Serb, or Macedonian and, at the same time, as a member of the larger political entity. Not only was dual identity possible; it was widespread. In the wake of Yugoslavia's disintegration, this historical lesson seems virtually lost on the national communities, who have opted to define their nation-states in terms of an exclusive ethnic identity, rather than an inclusive civic identity. For Slovenian citizens in particular, this lesson should be relearned and reformulated for the post-independence period. Considering their historic struggle to maintain an ethnic identity against the threat of being swallowed up in a larger ethnic frame, Slovenes, of all people, should understand the importance of sensitivity to the rights of ethnic minorities and the need for a multicultural competence. At the very least, the Slovenian notion of civic identity should fundamentally reject the "argument of size"—that is, the idea that the size of an ethnic community should ultimately determine whether or not it participates in international affairs. After all, this very argument has often been used in the past to deny the Slovene people's right to exist as a distinct national collective.

I hasten to add that having only a small number of people does not necessarily make a nation small. It is not being sentimental to say, moreover, that the "smallness" of a nation should be measured, first and foremost, by how much its citizens believe in the nation's creative potential and the richness of the shared cultural tradition—even if that tradition is increasingly accepted as "invented." The size argument, which holds that numerically small Slovenia must inevitably be absorbed into some larger political body, is often heard today, both in Ljubljana and in Brussels, the administrative seat of the European Union. Sadly, such claims are hardly new. A quick glance at Slovene history reveals the long tradition of this erroneous, if politically potent, argument. Such, for instance, was the so-called "Illyrian tradition" in the nineteenth century, promoted by the literary figures Stanko Vraz and Ljudevit Gaj, who called for the unification of the Slovene and Croatian languages out of a pragmatism that presumed the linguistic closeness of the two languages. After World War I, the size argument manifested itself in the ideological straightjacket of "integral Yugoslavism," which was advanced by the royal court and picked up after World War II by the communist authorities of the federal state, as Andrew Wachtel points out in his lucid book *Making a Nation, Breaking a Nation*. Today, the argument of size is often promoted by those members of the political elite who are incapable of understanding politics in the ancient Greek sense, as a discussion of public affairs, but rather view it merely as the technology of power. As such, they mistakenly believe that Slovenes can somehow be "unmediatedly" European, that is, without first being what they really are: citizens of the Slovenian nation-state. In other words, the fact that Slovenes are Europeans only insofar as they are citizens of the Slovenian nation-state, evaporates under the heat of the argument of size.

I am convinced, however, that the issue should be reversed. It was precisely the numerical smallness of the Slovene nation that compelled its key cultural figures to turn to foreign strategies of imagination and thought, assimilating these to their own local needs and conditions. The Slovenes' productive, if troublesome, geographic location at the crossroads of the Romance, Hungarian, Germanic, and Balkan cultural traditions made any bucolic Slovene homogeneity impossible. The concept of some self-absorbed, uncontaminated culture where the national *ego in Arcadia* could be quietly nurtured, is, of course, nothing but a mirage. Slovene creative thinkers have traditionally been engaged with the main currents of Western civilization, drawing freely from the Italian Renaissance, the Protestant Reformation (especially with its legacy of linguistic self-confidence), the Central European baroque, French rationalism, German Romanticism and expressionism, Viennese Art Nouveau architecture, British rock 'n' roll, and American pop art, not to mention the ubiquitous allure of the Hollywood screen and the intricacies of Balkan folk blues. Art and culture, if viewed only as some dispensable ornament to public life, can facilitate neither collective freedom nor the unfettered flight of the individual imagination. Art and culture would be doomed to a slow and gradual death if they provided nothing more than some ethnic decoration to the nation's political life. Josip Vidmar, Slovenia's leading literary critic in the period between the two world wars, captured the importance of local interaction with the tendencies of the larger world in *The Cultural Problems of Slovenian Identity* (1932). He vividly explained that a small nation is "like a very ragged peninsula—the ocean continually splashes against its many shores and a fresh wind forever blows across its entire surface."

Allegiance both to the "winds" of Central European sentiment and the "ocean" of the Western civilizing experience has helped me personally in two ways. As a literary artist using universal codes of expression to present a personal vision and as an ethnic Slovene with a particular collective experience in my background, I gradually learned to cherish intimations of difference, the pull of something that requires a reflective gait as it shifts over time as much as abstract ideas do, something that is, in this way, quite distinct from any locally fecund and palpable experience of space. Cosmopolitanism, as I see it, may lack the emotional appeal of a national identity, but it gains in its accomodation of a moral attitude: it is to a large extent a matter of ethical choice. This may very well be one of the main reasons why cosmopolitanism does not enjoy a widespread allure, but it must be pursued if our nation is to live meaningfully and in security and not merely survive. But, as Alberto Melucci observes in "Coexisting with Differences," cosmopolitanism

> also entails acceptance that we are not sufficient onto ourselves, that we are inseparably tied to the destiny of everyone else on this planet, and that only with them can we construct the world of dignity and humanity. But it entails, furthermore, that only if we are totally ourselves will we be able to do so. Cosmopolitan globalism and patriotic localism are therefore two inseparable faces of the present world situation, with a degree of tension that cannot be erased. (140–141)

Cosmopolitanism must thus be equipped with a multicultural competence, which means that one's mode of expression will, in fact, be enhanced by crossfertilization with other languages and cultural traditions. The legal frame for cosmopolitanism is to be found in the notion of civic identity. The conscious decision to embrace civic identity is quite different from simply enjoying "natural" ethnic identity, for it is based on a respect for differences and their active public articulation rather than merely on a liberal tolerance of different ethnicities and traditions. Liberal tolerance camouflages what is essentially something passive; it simply permits other different and diverse traditions to exist side by side. As such, it cannot be fully divorced from a self-congratulatory and highly patronizing attitude. Cosmopolitanism, however, actively links without attempting to unify. It thrives on an open-minded interest in other traditions. As such, it helps transform so-called natural, inherited, or genuine identities into a civic identity based on a common body of laws freely accepted by free and equal individuals. Such an acceptance of the rule of law can only be performed in modern, secular, democratic nation-states.

European Discontents

In post-communist Central and Eastern Europe, two kinds of parochialism attack the cosmopolitan attitude. The first emerges from a stubbornly autarkic, sometimes even very aggressive mentality that cannot and will not learn anything from others, much less accept them as part of the national public life. A second kind of parochialism comes from bona fide liberal "internationalists." They shy away from all aspects of the national cultural identity, recoiling in fear at the possibility of being lumped in with nationalist conservatives. As a result, they extend their uncritical approval to any idea that comes out of the West. Such people serve up an ingratiating *Gesundheit!* whenever one or another fashionable cultural guru sneezes in Paris, London, or New York.

The Velvet Revolutions of 1989, indeed, resulted in an apparent resurgence of the national idea throughout Central and Eastern Europe, rejuvenating debates about the validity of the collective experience while offering cheap promises of miraculous resolutions to the conflicts in the newly independent countries. More then a decade later, however, it has become rather clear that only a very few original approaches to the relationship between the national and global aspects of collective identity crystallized on the ruins of the communist *ancien régime*. Many intellectuals from Central and Eastern Europe have grudgingly accepted the role of "poor relatives" who must outdo each other in trying to impress their rich cousins in "Europe"—that is, in Western Europe.

But which Europe are we really talking about? On the one hand, the project of integrating diverse nations in an "ever closer" European Union should be viewed primarily as an economic and technological enterprise. As such, this goal is as interesting as it is inevitable. On the other hand, Europe can be regarded as a shared, if elusively shifting, cultural and mental landscape. At what price should the first view of Europe supersede the second? We should remember, too, that Europe today does not appear solely in the noble tradition of Greek philosophy, Roman jurisprudence, Renaissance humanism, Romantic poetry, or the politically crucial Enlightenment legacy of universal human and civil rights. Another aspect of the contemporary notion of Europe is increasingly being promoted in the populist right-wing politics of "Fortress Europe," "a barricaded society," and "fascism with a human face." Such staunchly conservative gatekeeping is presented as something that bolsters a perceived "natural" ethnic community, which one is either born to or excluded from—there is no third option.

Consider, for example, the nefarious connotation contained in a newly coined word for foreigners that has recently gained currency in Italy: *excommunitari*. This refers specifically to people who come from countries outside the European Union. In accordance with the labor laws, citizens of European Union member-states have long enjoyed the status of nationals throughout the Union; this has been most evident in the sports world, and especially in soccer. At the same time, however, an ever stricter policy has evolved in regard to the European Union's external borders. This newly fortified Europe, which seems so peace-loving within, looks quite different from outside. Citizens of countries that are not members of the Schengen Treaty—which, since July 1995, stipulates strict enforcement of a common border regime for all European Union members—by and large receive second-class treatment. They have a hard time getting entry visas and residency or work permits; they are kept in monitored camps on the new European borders; or they are briskly expelled. Dirk Schumer was entirely correct in his article "Modern Slavery" when he pointed out that long-standing historical, as well as more recent economic and political, reasons may make it difficult for Poland, once it enters the European Union, to accept more rigidly enforced borders with Lithuania and Ukraine. The same is true in regard to the Czechs and the Slovaks. Hungary's foreign policy since the 1920 Treaty of Trianon, this "peace without honor," has been steadily guided by concern for the whole of the Magyar people, which, of course, includes substantial Magyar minorities in neighboring Romania and Slovakia, as well as in parts of the former Yugoslavia.

The European Union's decision to adopt the strict Schengen Treaty line of external borders at a time when Central and East European candidate countries were waiting to join, has certain negative implications, especially in the way the European Union attempts to shift its own insecurities onto the shoulders of much weaker countries. The European enlargement process cannot avoid the issue of borders, though it would, of course, be nice to daydream about a borderless Europe. But the reality is that, while the borders are clearly defined on the west, north, and south sides of Europe, they are not at all clearly defined on the east side, that is to say, on Europe's soft underbelly.

Right-wing political parties are visibly making hay out of Europe's shifting borders, while liberal, left-wing, and centrist parties mostly watch in crippled bewilderment. All across Europe, political parties with programs directed against immigrants from outside the European Union have won significant public support recently. These include Pia Kjærsgaard's Danish People's Party in Denmark; Jorg Haider's Freedom Party in Austria; the House of Freedoms, the rightist alliance in Italy led by Silvio Berlusconi; the Spanish right-of-center People's Party; Jean-Marie Le Pen's National Front in France; and the Flemish Bloc in Belgium. Although these aggressive right-wing parties have but a few policy proposals in common, they all, at the very least, share the goal of making life extremely difficult for immigrants. Ideally, they would like to send immigrants back to their countries of origin and sharply limit the mixing of ethnic identities. What is more, while these parties inflame xenophobia, they do it without resorting to the kind of benighted provincialism that might provoke the public's outrage over their ethnic hate-mongering. In many instances, they even use tools provided by the European Union itself.

Instead of investing its joint efforts into creating a federal Europe that enjoys a high quality of life with adequate social safety nets, the European Union is becoming more and more like the "gated communities" one finds in the United States, where the inhabitants of wealthy neighborhoods keep their territory ethnically and socio-economically homogeneous by means of armed security guards, limited access, and astronomical real-estate prices. But what is happening in Europe is no cheap imitation of American urbanism or a result of American cultural pressure. Rather, it is an entirely domestic, entirely European response to a real challenge. We should remember that the regions of Europe which display the greatest resistance to foreigners are at the same time among the economically most successful—and most recently successful. Neither Austria nor Italy have anywhere near the number of immigrants as do, for example, such former colonial powers as Great Britain, France, and the Netherlands.

Such hatred of foreigners is, first of all, morally reprehensible. In the long run, however, it is also economically hazardous. Because of Europe's low birth rate, an unceasing influx of immigrants is necessary to maintain the necessary conditions for a high standard of living. European youth, the handicapped, the unemployed, and the ever increasing number of senior citizens depend on a shrinking labor force that will be unable, over the long haul, to support the current extent of medical and social services. According to many predictions, the deficit in the labor force over the next decade is likely to necessitate an increase in immigration to the European Union. Germany's politically broad-minded government program, launched in 2001, is designed to assuage this deficit by providing work and residency permits to foreign experts. In many sectors of the public, however, this program met with stiff resistance, offering a graphic illustration of the conflicting contemporary situation in European nation-states.

The essential feature of such conflicts is an opposition between a feeling of ethnic endangerment (immigrants threaten "our" values and social harmony) and economic needs (the German economy will languish without foreign experts). In short, ethnic fundamentalism—not only the notion of "Germanness," but also "Magyar essence," "Slovene identity," and "the Czech soul," etc.—collides with the neoliberal fundamentalism of the market. Meanwhile, the post-communist states of Central and Eastern Europe have themselves become destinations of choice for many foreigners. A large volume of immigration, both legal and illegal, now flows into these countries, especially from the territories of the former Yugoslavia and the former Soviet Union. Having failed to prepare for such large waves of immigration, these countries experience the shock of encountering people who are different and "other" all the more severely.

No less relevant is another consideration. After the fall of the Berlin Wall and the unification of Germany, after an accelerated economic integration among E.U. members and the successful introduction of a common currency—even after all these historic achievements, Western Europe still cannot conceal its political sterility. Indeed, the decay of its moral backbone was laid bare in a particularly excruciating way in the recent Balkan Wars, where European diplomacy for the most part attempted to deny Bosnian and Croatian victims the basic right to self-defense. The situation was painfully reminiscent of the 1930s, when Europe was still flaunting the arrogant authority of its "sick . . . secret diplomacy that trades in the territories of small nations and pacifies looks of rebellion by resorting to the League of Nations, where are seated the very people who sold these territories, the very people who tyrannize these lands," as the Slovene avant-garde poet Srečko Kosovel protested in his 1925 lecture "The Disintegration of Society and the Decline of Art." Kosovel was, of course, describing the situation in his own time, but his prophetic insight poetically intimates the situation today.

The Hidden Handshake

A responsible attitude toward the national tradition is essential. For in fact, culture is not a gift from our ancestors; rather, we have borrowed it from our own grandchildren. This claim is all the more true today, when the social conditions are less than promising. In Central and Eastern Europe, ethnic fundamentalism prioritizes a nasty "blood-and-soil" ideology while a haughty liberalism parrots the social-Darwinist logic of the global market. In his stimulating book, *Jihad vs. McWorld,* Benjamin Barber described these intertwined processes as, on the one hand, a mixture of hatred and the privileging of tribal comfort and, on the other, an all-embracing maximization of profit.

Despite a mutual hostility, populist movements based on ethnic, religious, or cultural exclusivism (Barber's ominous "Jihad") share many similarities with movements that propogate a "McWorld"—the uniformity and homogenization promoted by global corporations and transnational institutions such as the International Monetary Fund and the World Bank. The underlying idea of both is a dismissal of democracy. Jihad uses the bloody policy of ethnic chauvinism, while McWorld prefers the bloodless economy of profit. The former leads to an enforced blindness within which the traitors of the tribal "cause" are persecuted, while the latter offers a consumerist hedonism where we all do nothing but seek ever more adrenaline-pumping thrills. But neither the Jihad nor McWorld leave any room under their respective canopies for the citizen. This is Barber's most fruitful insight. While Jihad replaces the citizen with the paranoid warrior, McWorld cultivates the ignorant consumer. If the ancient truth, *si non est civis, non est homo,* still holds, then the consequences of acquiescing to either Jihad or McWorld will be premeditated catastrophe.

The emphasis on democracy is not accidental. Only a democratic order can guarantee a public sphere that offers the conditions for multiple identities and freely chosen cultural styles. It is, then, crucial to improve existing nation-state institutions—and, if necessary, develop new mechanisms—that foster the kind of identities that allow the individual to engage in *constitutional patriotism* regardless of his or her ethnicity, race, religion, or communal tradition. A civic identification with democratic nation-state institutions, one that is based on the rule of law and equal conditions for participation in public life, is the only possible buffer against the insidious forces of ethnic chauvinism. Ethnic identity is only one of the elements in a citizen's identity.

At the same time, citizenship in a democratic nation-state militates against the fanciful, but nebulous idea of being "citizens of the world," somthing that is often lauded as progressive. In contemporary international affairs, however, it is impossible to identify any democratically elected bodies that might actually represent individual citizens, rather than governments (as is the case with the United Nations). That is why it remains necessary to defend the idea of the democratic nation-state, which is based on a separation between national markers (in regard to the political state) and ethnic markers (relating to cultural background). In such states, citizens enjoy the right, though not necessarily the obligation, to organize their life according to their preferred cultural, religious, and political reserves of meaning. This is possible only when the public sphere is neither subsumed under the mantle of state institutions—and thus deprived of the creative and critical potential of a variety of lifestyles articulated outside governmental bodies—nor left entirely to the mercy of aggressive corporate interventions into the private and collective life-world, as John Keane argues in his essay, "Nations, Nationalism and European Citizens."

The democratic nation-state is important in that it regulates public life without dominating it. Zygmunt Bauman, possibly the most incisive theorist of postmodernity in the English-speaking world, in his book *Life in Fragments,* describes the predicament as follows: "The greater . . . is the share of nation-state sovereignty ceded to the all-European agencies, the less is the chance that the nation-state-based identities will be successfully defended." To dismiss the idea of the democratic nation-state means, ultimately, to usher in both a proliferation of fundamentalist groups and a celebration of the global capitalist machine, with its mind-numbing fast music, fast food, and fast computers. Allowing both processes to grow unhindered would in my opinion prove disastrous. The realms of Jihad and McWorld are, by definition, incapable of respecting the wholeness of the symbolic, cultural, and social experience that gives shape to collective mentalities. But if one does try to resist the temptations of market fundamentalism, then one may still find inspiration in the publicly negotiated meaning of the cultural tradition—with reservations, perhaps, but not without hope, and with the kind of dedication that refrains from glorification. Through such negotiations and struggles, one might just figure out where one stands, while attempting to decode the signals of our pre-catastrophic world, where entire nations are condemned to disappearance, as the tragedy of Bosnia, at least, attests.

My emphasis on language and cultural experience has, in the limited context of this chapter, but a single ambition: to dramatize the inherent dangers of the purely economic approach to national identity, which leaves art and culture completely at the mercy of market forces. The history of national culture cannot and should not be measured primarily according to its marketability, but rather according to the handshake of collective solidarity which draws its sustenance from the communal ligatures. If a people neglects this hidden handshake, it may very well turn into the kind of tribe of children H. G. Wells described in his futuristic novel *The Time Machine,* with no memory, no concerns and, by extension, no freedom. Wells's naïve tribe had no defense against the underground cannibalistic children of the dark—a vivid illustration of the calamitous consequences that befall a community when it loses a sense of its history, a sense of itself.

Chapter 2

Slovenia's Absence on the American Cultural Map

The aroma of cinnamon cappuccino wafted from an Italian café as the warm vibrations of the city filled my lungs. Fresh croissants called to me from a Polish bakery, a cluster of Rastafarians rolled an enormous joint right in front of everybody, an attractive black girl gazed at me seductively, a trumpet player standing on a corner near the Cooper Union building had just finished syncopating "Seems Like Old Times," and yellow cabs were racing by. It was just another miraculously ordinary day in New York, the capital of the twentieth century, to paraphrase the way an enthralled Walter Benjamin once described nineteenth-century Paris.

I admit I was gawking. I couldn't help it. When I came across my first homeless person on St. Mark's Place in the "radical-chic" East Village, I was horrified, shocked, bewildered. I had the unpleasant feeling that someone was watching me reproachfully to see whether I would turn a blind eye on such abject poverty and gingerly step over the human bundle. My Old World moral prejudices, steeped in the rapidly withering ideals of social democracy, were still with me. They had traveled across the Atlantic with me in the intellectual and emotional baggage I carried when, just a few days before, I first got off the plane in this "land of the free and the home of the brave." I was, of course, well aware, at least in theory, that I had come to a country where the glittering myth of success at any price, popular Horatio Alger stories about self-made men, and a heroic history of contempt for stifling social norms underpin the national mindset and, in particular, the possibly liberating yet dangerous belief that each person alone is responsible for his or her status in society.

For a newcomer from Slovenia and from the Yugoslav variety of "late communism" who on that early July afternoon in 1985 was about to enter the legendary St. Mark's Bookstore to seek refuge from a tumult of new impressions, the sight of the homeless man spoke volumes. The whole panorama of American self-reliance flashed through my mind in the single moment it took me to finally step over the helpless body in front of the bookstore. I tried to feign the same indifference I saw in the behavior of the other patrons, obviously locals, who were entering this citadel of culture.

Their casual air of self-involvement was something more than the ingrained habit of residents in an urban megalopolis; it was more than just a resigned shrug of the shoulders, as if to say: That's the way life is in late capitalism. Concealed within this reflex lay a deeper understanding of the contemporary human condition, one concerned less with the political economy of poverty than with the logic of the autonomous self. Indeed, this reflex was related to the metaphysical attitude that shapes the distinctive architecture of the American empire, which reigns over individual souls and collective mentalities alike both at home and in the modern "global village." With this matter-of-fact attitude, which even for me, a perplexed immigrant in New York, soon became something entirely ordinary, I quietly accepted the basic moral values inherent in such routine indifference toward the suffering of the others.

The first imperative one might discern in this attitude mirrors the same mentality that gives America its enormous appeal as the modern world's greatest secular myth, a country recognized throughout the globe as possessing a story worthy of (sometimes reluctant) emulation. What I am talking about is the imperative of *radical individualism,* which, at least in some of its extreme manifestations, might be associated with social Darwinism. That is to say, at issue is an invisible web of concerns and interests, ambitions and pleasures centered on the individual self—at least to the extent that the history of the pioneer conquest of the American West is founded on the determination of brave men and women to shape their own destiny and not be the playthings of historical forces or pawns in the political gambits of European despots. The pursuit of property and happiness—that most American of American values—is primarily the concern of one's individual self and should depend on neither king nor bishop.

Stories about men and women who burned all bridges, broke all ties with friends and family, and ventured into the unknown to stake their claim and start afresh, to make real some magical, ancient tale of winning success by the sweat of your brow, outside the strictures of traditional community life—such stories are the stuff American dreams are made of. Partly because of their redemptive impulse and moral absolutism, but mainly because they offer the potential for a multiple reinvention of the self, these dreams today animate and frustrate virtually the whole planet. At the same time, however, they leave little room for critical doubt or skeptical reservation, driven as they are by a conviction in the rightness of "doing one's own thing." Such dreams provide no place for an integral identity. How could it be any different? For these are dreams that feed on the ideal of a volatile, protean self. In such dreams, any sort of fixed, stable, or permanent self would too closely resemble the stifling bonds of tradition, rules, and routines, the very things Americans want to avoid.

Radical individualism, it seems to me, is part and parcel of an institution of national identification unlike any other in the world: a civil society and political state where anyone who wishes to can become an American. (It has to be said, alas, that since the terrorist attacks of September 11, 2001, young men with perceived Middle Eastern features seem less likely to be granted this privilege.) Still, the metaphysics of American self-reliance derive primarily from the historical impotence of the national tradition. In the proverbial melting pot of social and cultural difference, such a thing simply does not exist. Rather, what distinguishes the American cultural experience is the way in which German tenacity and Anglo-Saxon entrepreneurship, Protestant Puritanism, and Jewish intellectualism, Scandinavian fortitude and Italian sentimentality, Irish whimsy and African vitality, Chinese diligence and Latino *machismo* all complement each another with great, if too often troublesome, results.

Inspiration and the Paralysis of Cultural Heritage

From this perspective, we can understand why, apart from reliance on the self, an American finds his or her only other supports in a private allegiance to family and a civic devotion to the flag, the Bill of Rights, and the Constitution. In between lies a vast no-man's land of self-invention and freedom from the norms, values, and rituals of any larger community. This freedom must appear as a precious source of inspiration for realizing a most audacious and autonomous aspiration—autonomous in Thucydides' sense of the word: "He is autonomous, who himself conceives and establishes the law."

But this is only one aspect of the American condition. We must look, too, at the dark side of the American mind. Like the beautiful song of Homer's sirens, boundless freedom—not only geographic, but also mental and emotional freedom—not only seduces the American; at the same time, it threatens him with oblivion and anonymity. But the inevitable fragility of unique individual experience contravenes this slow surrender to the imperative of individualism. For a growing awareness of the transitory nature of individual endeavor, the mortality of human existence, and gnawing loneliness (which ultimately cannot be distinguished from a stubborn insistence on the protection of privacy) gives birth to an ever more palpable need for security—the kind of security the collective mentality can provide, however unstable or fictitious it might appear.

In America, an optimism of will and a pessimism of reason go hand in hand in search of a temporary home. Consider, for example, the contemporary American literary discourse, which relies on such notions as "women's writing," "the queer gaze," "African American heritage," "Native American poetry," "Chicano literature," and other collective identities that articulate the particular life of imagined communities, which in some ways resemble national identities. These politically acute and socially urgent forms of the collective imagination provide a surrogate home, however negotiated, for the American reader, exhausted by the excesses of late-twentieth-century radical individualism. Such categories offer a kind of existential shelter and a sense of emotional affinity—feelings, it would seem, which the legal ideals of the Constitution and the Bill of Rights cannot by themselves supply.

Let's take a random example. Toni Morrison's exciting, tragic, and complex 1977 novel *Song of Solomon* can be found on the shelves of American bookstores among other works by black writers. The label "African American Fiction" displayed on these shelves not only makes it easier and faster to find the author you want; it also signalizes a symbolic fact that is hard to overlook. It shows us that an authorial world acquires its full-blown image only in the larger context of a distinct cultural heritage—in Toni Morrison's case, African American ways of feeling and thinking. By this I mean not only earlier narratives in African American writing but also the conflicting social forces that gave birth to them, all of which made possible the construction of the aesthetic, moral, and ethnic framework within which Morrison's deeply personal literary voice was able to develop.

Certainly, the spirit of leftist politics, which thrived in the civil rights movement of the 1960s and dramatically changed the American political and cultural landscape, gave a crucial impetus to the emergence of various distinct literary traditions as it called for a greater public recognition of ethnic, gender, racial, and other kinds of minority rights. It would be short-sighted, however, to dismiss this awakening of particular identities as simply the incidental consequence of a certain "style of radical will," to borrow a phrase from Susan Sontag.

There are more profound existential reasons why the need arose to create frameworks of identification and stories about collective forms of experience that, on the one hand, transcend the perceptive power of the individual and, on the other, build it into a more stable mental structure and invest it with greater significance. These reasons might be found in the transhistorical need for a home, a space where everything has its name, and for an authentic totality in which one can be understood without having to explain the basic symbols one uses.

The Existential Need for a Home

One of the fundamental existential needs, not only of every artist, but of every human being is, I believe, the need to have one's personal vision fully expressed. That is to say, the words with which we create our vision must possess a meaning that is both comprehensive and detailed. For only then can our interlocutor or reader be truly enlightened, enriched, and broadened in experience; only then does communication become at all meaningful. I am convinced that the ivory-tower life of what Leibniz called "a monad without windows and doors"—a life of exclusively private experience that is not in dialog with any other experience—is solely the domain of ascetics and mystics, monks and hermits, who seek union with the divine in a way that refuses to submit to words.

But the rest of us want the thread of our words, unreliable, fragile, and transient though it may be, to speak to living beings of flesh and blood. We long for our poems and stories to bear witness, through their ethical force and aesthetic style, to some intimate vision of the time and space we inhabit. In the same breath, we hope that our vision of the cycle of life, whether it be anguished or joyous, will not only speak to those who share our ancestry, but will be able also to reach people of different backgrounds through the strength of its universal message. What drives us to write our poems and stories is a relentless yearning for our metaphors to speak about an individual destiny in such a way that, at least for a moment, it contains within itself everyone's destiny. The ritual of listening to tales is part of any primary collective, where words bear a crystal clear resonance because the listeners are familiar with their connotations and allusions and can thus participate in the shared heritage. We sense that the narrator's gifts and symbolic bonds to the community owe their extraordinary allure to the fact that they spring from an archaic cultural tradition, where stories told around the tribal fire embodied an absolute totality, so that when they were spoken, they were true.

Perhaps that is why today, in a world dominated by digital kitsch, an ever more select public is turning to the sanctuary of literature. For beneath the delicate arcade of a lyric poem or story, time stands still, making room for universal images of longing, horror, and love, in which we find endless stimulation for reflection on our own lives. This, in fact, may be the most precious gift art can offer. We therefore always need and, at the same time, presume a spontaneous ability to adapt and understand—an ability, I believe, that we assimilate only by belonging to some larger collective. Within the context of such a collective, the members help each other in both emotional and practical ways. They take part in community discussions, together shaping the public discourse and collectively making decisions, whether through unmediated interaction or with the help of some mutually accepted mechanism of mediation. In a word, the members of the larger collective share memory, history, and a living present, as Robert Bellah points out in *Habits of the Heart* (1985).

So then, to return my provisional example, the larger collective for contemporary black writers in America is the African American community, where memory of the painful history of slavery and racism is acutely felt. Authors who write from a personal perspective (and there's no other effective way to write) at the same time necessarily reflect in some way, perhaps vaguely, the measure and shape of their community as they make use of distant allusions and oblique references. In its raw, unprocessed, and unmediated psychological core, this web of intercommunication is likely to remain out of reach for the untutored and, indeed, for any reader who has not passed through the initiation rites needed to become a full-fledged member of the community. Such a reader will be at a loss to comprehend this linguistic web in all its illuminating and subtle details. But not only the devil dwells in these details, there is a god there, too, for details add up to more than their arithmetic sum. It is the overarching totality that alone can offer us a glimpse into the authorial universe's deeper currents of continuity, stability, and identity, which we continually try to discover in an aesthetically fruitful game of hide-and-seek.

Unless we have familiarized ourselves with the literary work of the Harlem Renaissance and Zora Neale Hurston's vivid folkloric accounts of life between the two world wars; unless we followed in the footsteps of the invisible man in Ralph Ellison's monumental novel, unless we have considered the legal consequences of the post–Civil War policy of a mule and forty acres and are conversant with the essays of W. E. B. DuBois and his searing critique of white supremacy; unless we have examined the syncretic aspects of African American Christianity in the antebellum South; unless we can empathize with the anguished hope that flickers through the novels of James Baldwin—in short, unless we have established an entire framework of historical and cultural references through which we glimpse a prismatic picture of the collective African American experience, it is impossible to enter fully into the world of Toni Morrison's novels.

I realize, of course, that it is Morrison's individual talent that gives us aesthetic pleasure, and it is her attentive ear for the magical dimension that helps her depict the struggle for survival in everyday African American life. Indeed, the artwork's redemptive universality resides precisely in its ability to draw parallels and analogies in subtly ambiguous ways, so that even in a novel about experiences radically different from our own we recognize the universal human emotions of sorrow, pain, and love.

I have read too many books on phenomenology and deconstruction to make the naïve claim that it is possible to penetrate a literary work to its innermost depths. Clearly, access to a single incontestable truth is impossible thanks to the tensions that exist between such layers of signification as structure, rhythm, word choice, and quasi-real events. All this I know well. I am not talking about the ultimate truth of the literary work but rather about the conditions needed for a comprehensive perception of its potential meanings. Within this narrow perspective, I seek to touch the emotional, conceptual, historical, and metaphysical worlds that open to me through a sensitive reading, on the one hand, and, on the other, through my empathy for the collective group that gave rise to the individual authorial vision.

In this regard, I suspect that Morrison's *Song of Solomon* reveals itself to a reader from the African American community in a way quite different—more profound, perhaps, and more compelling—from how it reveals itself to me, a white non-American. But I must quickly add, I do not think this way is necessarily more "correct." Ever since Wilhelm Dilthey analysed the hermeneutic horizon of understanding, we have been free of the burden of ideological reading, for we have learned that in matters of artistic discourse one cannot speak of right and wrong. Still, I think it fair to say that an African American reader who shares the same emotional memory, historical links, local archetypes, and metaphysical symbols as Morrison and her protagonists will experience a degree of identification, consolation, and inspiration in *Song of Solomon* that is almost certainly beyond reach for those of us who are, in the literal sense of the word, "other."

I should stress, however, that I in no way advocate the sort of essentialist position that emerged in the early 1980s, arguing zealously that (to put it bluntly) only African American professors could interpret African American literature since they have a more immediate, intimate, and ipso facto "authentic" relationship with the material. If that were the case, no one could possibly dis-·cuss Sophocles' tragedies or the moral dilemmas they disclose even today with undiminished power. The absurdity of essentialism is obvious at least on cognitive level. Here I want to say only that primary identification derives from the primary collective, which represents the first, although not necessarily the best, form of security and meaning.

Secular Myths

In the contemporary American context, primary collectives are based on ethnic, racial, or gender difference. In the context of contemporary Central and East Europe, the primary collective is still—despite increasingly vocal regional iden-tifications—more or less founded on national difference. Modern national iden-tity as an ideal type, understood in Max Weber's sense, represents that form of collective identity in which people, who may or may not be in physical contact or personally know each other, view their mutual affiliation and commitment as binding for several reasons: because they share a common language or dialect; because they live together in the same geographic area or have an intimate con-nection with the land and relate to its ecosystem with a good deal of emotional enthusiasm; and because they participate in a number of common customs, in-cluding public rituals that memorialize their history.

National identity, thus defined, is a European invention. As John Keane ob-serves in his inspiring essay "Nations, Nationalism, and European Citizens" (1995), the political, if not metaphysical, meaning of national identity lies pri-marily in its ability to give members of a collective group

> a sense of purposefulness, confidence and dignity by encouraging them to feel
> "at home." It enables them to decipher the signs of institutional and everyday
> life. The activities of others—the food they prepare, the products they manu-
> facture, the songs they sing, the jokes they tell, the clothes they wear, the looks
> on their faces, the words they speak—can be recognized. That familiarity in
> turn endows each individual with a measure of confidence to speak and to act.
> (186)

This inner condition of self-evident familiarity with the faces and rituals, songs and secular myths of the collective can be found, too, in the instinctive confidence manifested in one's mother tongue. In this regard, it is probably jus-tified to say that, for example, only a Slovene reader can grasp, in all its sym-bolic connotations, a poem such as Tomaž Šalamun's "Duma" [Meditation], written in 1964. Here Šalamun, then a young avant-garde poet, presents a witty parody of another "Duma," written nearly sixty years earlier by Oton Župančič, one of the founding fathers of modern Slovene poetry. Šalamun did not choose his target randomly. Slovene schoolbooks indelibly imprint the minds of young readers with a distinctly Slovene secular myth that finds its supreme expression in the Župančič poem.

The 1908 poem, structured around the proud exclamation, "I walked through our land and drank its delights," embodies a mythic love of the landscape that is based on the premodern archetype of the innocent nature. In Župančič's dated but nevertheless aesthetically skillful language, this archetype, on the one hand, highlights fidelity to the peasant heritage, while, on the other hand, it skips over the lack of cultural achievements, which the Slovenes, as a stateless nation, had to postpone in their historic struggle for national survival. Obviously, only the Slovene reader can discern in Šalamun's mockery of the canonized poem those levels of collective representation that help Slovenes piece together the symbolic economy of nationality.

Šalamun's "Duma" ironically rewrites the famous Župančič line as, "I walked through our land and got a stomach ulcer," and so criticizes the focus of Župančič's grandiose epic ambition. At the same time, Šalamun plays with assumptions of national self-confidence, that is, with the "raw material" of patriotic cultural history—the kind of thing we see in early-twentieth-century Slovenian postcards with their gushing pride in the landscape; the idyllic recollections of family harmony in the widely reproduced paintings of Maksim Gaspari (a sort of Slovene Norman Rockwell); the exuberant naïveté of early tourist brochures; and so on. Such long-established symbolic forms, which have historically enchained Slovene attitudes and modes of thought, are thus subjected to critical reappraisal in the later poem.

Šalamun's poetic gesture is, indeed, much more than just youthful play with a literary classic; it presupposes a change in the vocabulary of spatial perception. The perceptive Slovene reader is forced to think about forms of national identity—and national identity is never simply a given but is rather both the object and the outcome of conflicting interpretations that together produce the image of a nation, the "imagined community," as Benedict Anderson puts it. The Slovene reader, then, will almost be obliged to notice that both "Duma" poems play an important role in shaping modern Slovene national identity. The fact that Župančič and Šalamun both make reference to nature shows how symbols are disputed in the unending negotiation of different interpretations, which only in their totality create sites of national memory. As combative, and sarcastic as Šalamun might be in his opposition to constrictive national formulas—personified for him in Župančič's patriotic enthusiasm and the primary collective tradition that codifies it—his own aesthetic language is nevertheless unmistakably informed by his rebellious stance toward that same tradition. Negation is also a form of determination.

The tradition of the primary collective carries weight not only for Slovene writers. Even if we look at Salman Rushdie, an eternal immigrant who has built his whole identity as a writer on the overcoming of borders and the rejection of any exclusive linguistic or national tradition, we find that most Western readers, upon encountering his epic canvases, see in them little more than fictional worlds and the charm of skillful legerdemain. But readers on the Indian subcontinent—Rushdie's cultural homeland and the setting for most of his novels—readily (and properly, as the author remarked in his 1991 essay "Imaginary Homelands") detect political critique as well, a hidden commentary on the real-life course of history and a courageous attempt to interpret the turmoil of Indian and Pakistani society.

I am, of course, familiar with the theory Harold Bloom set forth in his seminal work *The Anxiety of Influence* (1975). Misreadings, he argued, can harbor fruitful potential, disclosing in textual elements liberating vistas that remain hidden to one who reads solely from the point of view of a given collective tradition or a genre's origins. I do not question Bloom's thesis. But here I am primarily interested in an aspect of reading that Bloom necessarily overlooks but that can be of crucial importance in understanding a particular literary work, at least to the extent that it guides the reader through a web of allusions into a primary cultural frame.

Consider, for instance, the wrenching emotional dynamics of Niko Grafenauer's "Crngrob" (1984), perhaps the most moving work in contemporary Slovene lyric poetry. Written in a style inspired by Paul Célan but nonetheless thoroughly personal, this elegy is structured around broken verses that eloquently underscore clusters of meaning. But these clusters cannot be truly understood unless the reader is familiar with the history of Nazi-occupied Slovenia and, in particular, with the civil war between the communist-led Partisan resistance and the anticommunist Home Guard. The reader must know something, too, about the bloody revenge Tito's Partisans exacted on members and sympathizers of the Home Guard whom the Allies sent back to Slovenia at the end of World War II. A reader unfamiliar with the tragedy of Slovenia's civil war will in some critical way not be able to share in the sublime existential pain of Slovene history, which is the core element of "Crngrob."

Contemporary Slovene literature is replete with examples that reveal the essential bond between individual literary expression and local cultural tradition: Miloš Mikeln's novel *The Big Dipper* [Veliki voz] (1992), with its extended chapters on the peasant origins of both the bourgeois salon and the revolutionary spirit in twentieth-century Slovenia; Marjan Tomšič's numerous novels in which the author lovingly unearths the folklore, exotic even for Slovenes, linked to the magic traditions of the multicultural Istrian penninsula; Lojze Kovačič, born in Basel, Switzerland, to a Slovene father and German mother, a so-called orphaned post–World War II writer who has produced stunning autobiographical prose, urban chronicles composed with merciless honesty and the precision of an accountant.

Only Slovenes can understand the national framework of the Slovene literary and cultural tradition in an integral way—the way one understands one's own body: intuitively, reliably, efortlessly. Literary and (especially) poetic inspiration, springing from the depths of the self and filtering through the mean-dering streams of collective history, is nothing more than a "psychosomatic condition," as the Polish poet Anna Swir so accurately described it. Even when two sweat-drenched bodies are, in the same fraction of an endless second, hurled toward an erotic climax of trembling pleasure, they nevertheless do not achieve the same orgasm; always, there are two, and, despite our best efforts, each of us remains alone.

Are the Borders of My Language the Borders of My World?

It may be that this sense of being alone is all the more intense when you are in a foreign country; for me, at least, it is a torturous dilemma. Writers who work in a language spoken by a small number of people—such as Slovene, with only two million speakers—find that this dilemma follows them wherever they go, an ever-recurring fact of reality. The core question is this: If it is absolutely neces-sary to share in the collective mentality in order to have a rich and truly compre-hensive experience of a literary work, does that mean I am condemned to remain within the limits of my language, which are at the same time the limits of my symbolic, historical, and social worlds, as Ludwig Wittgenstein stated?

This dilemma percolated my mind that afternoon in early July when I fi-nally did manage to step over the homeless man and into St. Mark's Bookstore. Before my astonished eyes there opened a sea of books, splashing onto display windows, cascading off tables, books everywhere, tottering precariously on the shelves in this microcosm of American literary life. For a few intoxicating hours I lost myself in this splendid abundance, as any avid reader can easily imagine. But those who can remember the moment of their physical initiation into the world of books, when books they could only dream about became material real-ity in their trembling hands—such readers will have a much better idea of what I felt as I stood amid the mounds of titles. For years, filled with admiration and envy, I read about the delights of the writing life in *The New York Review of Books*, to which I subscribed as a way of appeasing, in distant Ljubljana, my voracious need for new aesthetic and literary galaxies and my craving for the apparently inaccessible horizons of the New World.

After a few delightful hours of leafing through books, skimming backspines and authors' names, running my hands over the laminated covers, after a few hours that went by as quickly as a shooting star, I stopped—and not only out of a sweet fatigue. I was beginning to realize that, if I didn't want to burn out, I would have to devise some plan to help me negotiate the bookshelves. I would have to find a reference point so as not to lose my way in the bewildering laby-rinth. For the bookstore had in my mind assumed a certain Borgesian quality, with doppelgänger and mirror images, especially in the light of that feeling of infinity you get when, for a fleeting moment, you see yourself in someone else's poem or story; life takes on a certain independence, acquiring a full, resonant voice that you yourself cannot provide. That, indeed, is what readers search for endlessly in poems and stories.

In the end, it was the poetry section that drew me to itself. At that time, like most poets at the beginning of the writing life, I euphorically imagined that poetry was my true motherland: only within its geography and history was I really at home. Surely it was only in the fragile palaces of poetry that one could find the primordial text of life, ready to give up its secrets. Surely it was poetry alone, with its strange and beautiful simplicities of tender feeling and throbbing pain, that could tune my heart to the grace and wisdom born where spiders weave their webs in silence, in the gutters of rotting dreams, to paraphrase the Nigerian British writer Ben Okri. And because its social marginality makes it commercially irrelevant in today's corporate world, only poetry could freely uncover the fear and hope that reside in those corners of the heart where only desperate adventurers dare go.

Such is poetry's alluring power, such is its evansescent dignity as an art discipline that has seen its public dwindle almost to nothing in a century that began with the horror of dismembered bodies and ended in spiritual emptiness. And such is the poet's obligation, at least for those of us who recognize the urgent need for poetic memory and are able, at the beginning of our creative lives, to pronounce our *credo qui absurdum est.* Nevertheless, I am ever more firmly convinced that what Octavio Paz calls poetry's *other voice*—that is, the ability of poetic discourse to name the unknown even as it brings it into being— achieves full expression only when we can perceive it in relation to something already known.

When I stand before the cathedral at Chartres, admiring its slender towers, luminous stained-glass windows, and fantastic figures, I cannot help but seek in them the same forms, raised to their highest potential, that beckoned to me every day from the little country churches of my childhood, which were built by itinerant stonemasons. In a similar way, I try to understand the secret of *das ganz Andere*—that absolute reality that is entirely other and which in our secular age resides only in art—by automatically translating it into something I know, comparing and juxtaposing it to the images of my primary socialization and the cadences of my mother tongue. That is to say, I turn for help to images that were imprinted on my mind by the experiential map of childhood, the most reliable touchstone for an artist.

On the one hand, then, lyric poetry is wedded to the mother tongue. (Divorces, of course, can happen, but they seldom improve the partners.) For a poet, the native language is, indisputably, of primary importance. Czesław Miłosz, for instance, even after living thirty years in Northern California, never in his poetry yielded to the dangerous temptation of exchanging his native Polish for the more ecumenical reach of American English, despite possible career advantages. While there are a number of excellent twentieth-century expatriate writers (Samuel Beckett, Emile Cioran, Vladimir Nabokov, Milan Kundera, etc.) who successfully switched to the language of their adopted countries, these are themselves exceptions that prove the rule, and significantly, they are known primarily for prose, not poetry. A true poet is born into his native language, its burden and inspiration. On the other hand, there is the no less important fact that all the formative events through which the *genius loci* is expressed—symbolic, historical, military, political, social, and metaphysical—lie buried in the layers of the national language, suggesting a more or less hidden anchorage in national tradition.

Examples are easy to find. The Irish cultural tradition reverberates, if only in negation, throughout the radical compositional and linguistic experiments of James Joyce. To fully assimilate John Ashbery's sumptuous poetic work, one must read it against the philosophical and stylistic horizons created by Wallace Stevens and, before him, by Walt Whitman. Even the melancholy refinement of Adam Zagajewski's poetry, such as in his collection *Tremor* (1985), can be fully understood only when read in the opressive light of twentieth-century Polish cultural and political history. That is to say, we must consider not only its relationship to Miłosz, but also its background of confrontation, muffled dissent and, ultimately, solitary grief in regard to Poland's communist regime and the loss of Zagajewski's native city, Lvov, to the Soviet Union in the post-war division of the Polish borderlands.

Isolation and Identification

When I made for the poetry section at St. Mark's Bookstore, I was involuntarily seeking a double frame of reference for self-identification: not only poetry in general, but also writing from the Slovene national tradition. So what did I find for this second frame of reference? Nothing. Literally nothing. I faced a devastating emptiness. For there, amid the shiny bindings that held the verses of St.-John Perse, John Keats, Arthur Rimbaud, Omar Khayyam, Rainer Maria Rilke, Mahmud Darwish, Rumi, Pablo Neruda, Mark Strand, Fernando Pesõa, Allen Ginsberg, Sándor Weöres, Derek Mahon, Johannes Bobrowski, Vasko Popa—there, where the best of Slovene poetry should stand shoulder to shoulder with these lyric masters, I found nothing but a painful, gaping void.

There in St. Mark's Bookstore, on a brilliant New York afternoon, I felt for the first time just how alone I was and, in a certain essential way, how alone Slovenes as a nation are. Loneliness, after all, is not the absence of others, but the awareness that others do not understand what you say. I felt my cheeks burning, a tingling up and down my spine, my knees growing wobbly. I had to brace myself against the bookshelf; in the pit of my stomach I felt the curse of Slovene self-doubt. I realized with a sense of dread that I was under the spell of our collective self-consciousness, that I, too, suffered the traumatic consequences of living in that small republic between the Alps and the Adriatic Sea among a people inwardly violent and outwardly docile, with one of the highest suicide rates in the world.

The literary works that get translated into English include all kinds of contemporary writers, from every corner of the globe, but Slovenes are not well represented. Or rather, to be brutally honest, Slovene writers are almost completely unknown to the American reading public. There is but one exception.

Although I soon became a regular visitor to New York bookstores, I had to wait until 1988 to find a book in which American readers could discover for the first time the Slovene creative imagination: *The Selected Poems of Tomaž Šalamun*, from Ecco Press. From the dust jacket there gazed at me the heavily shadowed face of the poet who transformed the status and structure of poetry in my native land when, some thirty years ago, he published his groundbreaking book, *Poker* (1966). Influenced by the French *poètes maudits* and the radical linguistic experiments of the Russian poet Velemir Khlebnikov, his work has had a staggering impact on several generations of Slovene neo-avant-garde poets who have sought to follow Šalamun into a hermetic paradise filled with gnostic truths and unrestrained "trans-rational" language. Before Šalamun, Slovene poets could not even think about such things in any articulate way.

In Ecco Press selection of his poetry, edited by Charles Simic, I sought support against the ever more depressing realization that, as a poet, I was utterly alone on the North American continent. I had a growing awareness of being the unwilling victim of a paradox. On one hand, in the Babylonian bustle of postmodern New York, I kept hearing a hollow echo from the depths of my national poetic tradition, an echo of Josip Murn's description of the poet as *a poplar all alone*—an image that had been very important for my poetic formation. On the other hand, I knew in my heart that I had come to New York to find out whether or not as a poet I could transcend the gravitational pull of this metaphor and extricate myself from the straitjacket of parochial thought.

In a strange transference, this state of unrequited love might best be expressed by the words on a copper memorial plaque affixed to a brownstone house just a few doors away from St. Mark's Bookstore: "If equal affection cannot be / Let the more loving one be me." These lines, famously, belong to W. H. Auden, who once lived in that house. They could easily describe the feelings of the many poets and writers who today stream into New York, seeking confirmation for their poems and ideas, just as in the early twentieth century numerous artists left their provincial capitals on a pilgrimage to Paris. For thanks to America's cultural domination of the globe today, New York is where the fate of the world's art is decided for better or for worse.

Recognizing the paradox of "unequal affection," I had no choice but to accept with a bitter grin the definition of the poetic vocation that Murn had provided at the dawn of Slovene literary modernism, an image of shimmering beauty that conveys the truth of poetic solitude. For me, this lonely poplar tree was more than just aesthetic code for the individual voice in a clamorous age; it conveyed the internalized history of the Slovene creative quest. In Šalamun's book, I tried to find support for my illusion of being "at home" in poetry: first, in this concrete, if minuscule, image of Slovene presence in an American context, and second, in the lyrical substance of the Slovene national tradition as it was critically examined under the spotlight of Šalamun's imagination. I was, indeed, seeking in his book a substitute for the kind of frame of reference that is readily available to writers who work within larger, richer, and better-known national cultural traditions.

But even with Šalamun, American readers seemed to require a supplementary filter. A nameless blurb-writer described Šalamun on the dust-jacket flap as a "Yugoslav poet who writes in Slovene." There was, of course, nothing wrong about that simple statement of fact. However much Slovenes wish today to distance themselves from the other Southern Slavs, the seventy-year Yugoslav period is undeniably a major segment of Slovene history.

In the mid-eighties, only the most perceptive and informed Western observers could detect the first fissures in the political edifice of Yugoslavia. And even then it was hardly possible to foresee the outbreak of the new Balkan Wars, which in 1991 ended Slovenia's common life with its South Slavic cousins and led to the horrific devastation perpetrated by Serb battalions in Croatia, Bosnia, and Kosovo. But Slovenes, in a kind of inverted inferiority complex, like to think of themselves as somehow set apart from other Yugoslavs. That tiny biographical note on the back cover of Šalamun's American book dealt a humbling blow. To be precise, it relegated Slovene cultural tradition to the lower branches of the European family tree, rubbing shoulders with other stateless peoples such as Basques, Welsh, Scots, Lapps, Catalans, and Bretons. But whether or not Slovenes admit it, that is precisely where we were before the national independence.

There are two possible explanations for this situation. The first, heard quite frequently today in Slovenia, is based on a logic of dominance, specifically, the dominance of the Serbs in the life of communist Yugoslavia. It goes something like this: As the most numerous ethnic group, the Serbs were able to manipulate the various mechanisms of state promotion in international diplomatic, political, and cultural circles in ways that privileged their own creative works. As a result, it was not easy for the literature of other nationalities in the former Yugoslavia to penetrate the quasi-official Serb filter.

This is probably true. But at the same time, we need to consider the second explanation, less often voiced but no less relevant, namely, that the Yugoslav context played a beneficial, if somewhat ambiguous, role in the promotion of Slovene writers. This context assured potential readers, at least on a superficial level, that a writer like Šalamun came from a culture that had already given the world a few famous literary names: for example, the Nobel Prize winner Ivo Andrić, who wrote such masterful chronicles of Balkan life as *The Bridge on the Drina;* Danilo Kiš, who won international acclaim for his depiction of the terrors of history in, among other things, *A Tomb for Boris Davidovich;* and Vasko Popa, who grafted the rich tradition of Serbian folklore on audacious surrealist poetry in *Earth Erect.* In other words, thanks to the the Yugoslav context, Šalamun's selected poems were not left hovering in some referential limbo.

This does not mean, of course, that Šalamun, had he lacked a recognizable national context, would not have become what he is today, a major figure in contemporary international poetry, making regular appearances at leading poetry festivals from Jerusalem to Toronto to Rotterdam. Indeed, his works have been translated into numerous European languages and received significant praise, as attested, for example, by Kevin Hart's comprehensive review essay in *Verse* (2001). But it would probably have taken him much longer to acquire this reputation without the Yugoslav context, if he had been compelled to rely only on the American-style radical individualism he took as a model. His life and art, in fact, are so closely interwoven with the energy of the New World that one of his numerous poetry books bears the title *America*. For Šalamun, the Yugoslav frame provided nothing more than the first step to worldwide acclaim. Significantly, in making his breakthrough into the American and international literary arenas, he could not refer to any Slovene context, for none existed outside Slovenia itself. And that is still pretty much the way things stand today.

Recognizing the Cultural Context

There is, however, yet another way to look at the cultural context offered by the former Yugoslavia. For Slovene writers in the 1950s, 1960s, and 1970s, when travel abroad was still difficult and the limits on communication between Yugoslavia and the West were still daunting, getting translated into Croatian, Serbian, or Macedonian was a legitimate, if not perfect, surrogate for reaching the "outside world." The fact that Slovene literature was reaching Yugoslav readers in Zagreb, Sarajevo, Belgrade, and Skopje helped soothe the feeling of national isolation. In the Yugoslav frame, most of the important works of Slovene literature found interested readers beyond the Slovene borders. Indeed, these readers could explore our literature beyond the standard translated classics thanks to a multitude of small publishers, special book series, magazines, and anthologies, which frequently published Slovene writing. As a result, today Croatian, Macedonian, and Serbian readers undoubtedly know Slovene literature better than anyone else outside of Slovenia.

This should not be forgotten even now, when all eyes in this little Central European country are hypnotically fixed on the "paradise lost" of Europe. Since Yugoslav translations of Slovene literature took place more or less systematically, the full scope of this generous process was not readily apparent at the time. Only now, when the Yugoslav context has ceased to exist, can we evaluate both its limitations and advantages. And only now can we understand, for instance, why older Slovene writers by and large do not have, next to their Serbian, Croatian, and Macedonian translations, books translated into the languages of Western Europe: under the restrictions of communist system, there were only limited opportunities for such translations, but neither was there any sense of an urgent need for them.

Not so long ago, then, Slovene literature did enjoy a broader cultural context: the Yugoslav context. Gradually, however, various appetites for political power began to metastasize, until in the late 1980s the skeletons fell out of the common state closet as a single national group—the Serbs—sought control over the others. It soon became clear that respect for "the other" and the right of national groups to express themselves in their own way had little or no meaning for the national communists in Belgrade, who were for too long led by the now-indicted war criminal, Slobodan Milošević.

In the early 1980s, a different broader context began to make itself felt. In 1984, in an essay published in *The New York Review of Books* called "The Tragedy of Central Europe," Milan Kundera issued a passionate call to acknowledge the common historical experience of the former Habsburg lands—the experience of small victimized nations trapped between the self-involved West and the despotic East. Though hardly anyone today is engaged in a vigorous and far-reaching debate over the notion of Central Europe, this call for recognizing the larger common cultural frame seemed extremely liberating in the 1980s. It provided a welcome impetus for Slovene literary culture, which was trying to shake off the Serb-dominated Yugoslav context and place itself in another cultural context, one that would, hopefully, be more amiable and more supportive of autonomous growth.

My generation of writers, who came of age in the 1980s, had few illusions about either of these larger broader contexts. We could discard the once cozy but now ever more suffocating cloak of Yugoslavism more easily than our older Slovene colleagues, while we wore our Central European culture lightly, like a jaunty cap of pride, that is to say, as a mark of self-esteem that was necessary but hardly sufficient in itself. In the early 1990s, newly independent Slovenia was still celebrating its birth and had no trouble allocating funds for the cultural sphere—unlike today, when neoliberal economic pragmatism holds sway. The Trubar Fund was established to foster the translation of Slovene literature into other languages. Later, several books appeared in collaboration with British and American publishers who had developed an interest in contemporary Slovene literature. These included the 1993 anthologies, *The Day Tito Died: Contemporary Slovenian Short Stories* and *The Double Vision: Four Slovenian Poets*. Around the same time, the Vladimir Bartol Fund was set up, with meager start-up capital and enormous enthusiasm, to provide systematic assistance for Slovene writers to promote their work abroad, to fund translations from Slovene, and to keep track of Slovene writing in translation. All this goes to show that for writers of my generation there was no longer any real dilemma about where to look for the larger context: it was the "global village."

Not New but Eternal

But even with such efforts, Slovenes cannot simply close their eyes and hope the legacy of Yugoslavia will just disappear—the way so many villages and towns disappeared in the wars of the 1990s. The same is more or less true in regard to the political and social heritage of communism. It would be utterly naïve to think we could put it in historical brackets. There is no use pretending that communism was nothing more than an accidental, if lengthy, nightmare, which Central and Eastern Europe finally woke up from in the Velvet Revolutions of

1989. Nor should we think it possible to return to some pre-communist society. What a mistaken illusion! The communist heritage will be with us for some time, since it not only colonized our institutional arrangements, and the fabric of society in general, but, most of all, it established itself in the habits of our hearts and minds in a way that cannot be easily dismantled, as the public monuments to disgraced leaders have been.

In any case, communism provided the Western reading public with an immediately recognizable frame of reference. Whatever price writers paid for such basic recognition, it meant that Slovenes belonged to the much larger communities of Yugoslavia and communism. Of course, this required literary works to employ pain and melancholy, decrepitude and resistance, all of which stirred the Western reader. My friend and fellow writer Andrej Blatnik, author of the exquisite short story collection *Skinswaps,* would say, with some justification, that the Western literary market, forever on the lookout for the unknown and the exotic, likes to "import suffering." And although I agree that this is a factor in the logic of the book trade and should not be disregarded, the tariff on imported suffering is paid only once, in the first attempt at winning the attention of Western readers and critics.

On the second go-round—that is, once a presence in the international arena has been established—the main thing that counts is a highly individualized imagination: the depth and originality of the aesthetic world the writer presents to the reader. Ismail Kadare, Zbigniew Herbert, Ivan Klima, Péter Esterházy, Evgeny Popov, Norman Manea: I cannot believe that the appeal these modern Central and East European writers hold for Western readers rests solely on the fact that they describe certain historical curiosities or that the length of their popularity depends solely on external political events. In order to achieve international success and sustain interest, these writers had to create coherent literary worlds that revealed multilayered images of integral experience—not only historical but also metaphysical—intertwining aesthetic and ethical concerns in ways that differ from Western writing. For these Central and East European authors present us, ultimately, with different moral struggles, different national cataclysms, and different emotional involvements.

Such writers demonstrate, each in his or her own personal style, that in order to create art that survives its age it is not enough to chase after new trends that die as soon as the flocks of third-rate writers get hold of them. Art that is faithful to its existential purpose embodies nothing less than the longing to transcend human mortality. This is what readers seek in the kind of literary work that endures long after the rest of its contemporaries have been recycled to pulp: not something new, but something eternal.

Let us consider for a moment the experience of reading Milan Kundera. Do we not see in his novels and essays certain stylistic twists that allude to the dreamlike realism of Franz Kafka? Can we not perceive Kundera's mooring in the music of Smetana and Janáček, the philosophical ingenuity of the Prague Linguistic Circle, the legacy of Czech surrealism, and even the democratic scope of Tomáš G. Masaryk's political thought? Can we not clearly see Kundera's connection to the Czech tradition of traumatic existence and ironic resistance? We could argue endlessly about the degree and gravitational pull of the writers, artists, composers, and thinkers who serve as sources for national cultural inspiration. But it is a fact that all the Czech cultural figures I just mentioned are known, at least superficially, to Western intellectuals, better journalists, university professors, and graduate students of literature—there exists in the West a frame of reference for Czech culture. Such an assumption, however, could hardly be made for the Slovene cultural tradition. To quote the Slovene novelist Ivan Cankar, "I paint darkness so the eye might long more deeply for light."

The Peculiarities of Literature

For the record, I should mention that certain Slovene artists and writers have in fact enjoyed a measure of success in the international cultural context. A few names have managed to attract the attention of international cultural consumers despite the lack of a recognizable collective frame.

First of all, there is the architect Jože Plečnik, who redesigned Prague's Hradčany castle in the period between the two world wars; he was forced to retreat to private life after World War II, but recently, European and American publishing houses have issued serious monographs about him and he is enjoying a surge of worldwide interest. Then there is the avant-garde art collective Neue Slowenische Kunst, which includes both the techno-industrial rock band Laibach and the conceptual art group Irwin. For a number of years, the sculptor Marjetica Potrč has been showing her work in one respected international exhibition after another, and in 2001 was awarded the prestigious Hugo Boss Award, which included a show at the Guggenheim Museum in New York. The wildly acclaimed "stand-up" philosopher Slavoj Žižek—with numerous books, international lecture tours, and the editorship of a prestigious book series for the London publishing house Verso—has established himself among the world's leading thinkers. From his Paris home, the blind photographer and writer Evgen Bačar disseminates his sublimely nostalgic vision of Central Europe. In the realm of theater, the energetic director Matjaž Pograjc can surely count on continued international recognition for his performing troupe Betontanz, as can the theater director Tomaž Pandur, a master of the lush postmodern spectacle. Among fiction writers, one must mention Drago Jančar, Slovenia's preeminent novelist, whose works include *Mocking Desire* and *Northern Lights;* Boris Pahor, a Slovene from Trieste whose novel *Pilgrim Among the Shadows* is among the finest works to come out of the horrors of the Holocaust; Evald Flisar, who spent many years in Great Britain and Australia and is the author of *My Father's Dreams;* and Brina Svit, who has lived in Paris some twenty years and whose recent novel *Con Brio* has won her an international readership—all of these books have recently been published in English translation.

Although more people could be named, the list would still be pathetically short. The important accomplishments by Slovenes in the international cultural and intellectual arenas, together with a few scattered works from Slovene artists of the past, have failed to cohere into a wide-cast net of recognition that would signify the unmistakable Slovene presence on the cultural map of the world. I should also note that the comprehensive *Historical Dictionary of Slovenia* was published in London in 1996, but it is intended primarily for scholars, not for the general educated reader.

Slovene literature finds itself in a predicament even more discouraging than that of the other arts. Because it is uniquely bound to the mother tongue, literature cannot rely on the support structures available to other artistic disciplines. It cannot make use of the universal patterns of line, color, and volume that allow a viewer, even on first inspection, to place a work of visual art, at least approximately, within the rhythmic succession of international styles. Nor can it make use of the universals of popular music—neither the standard arrangement of guitar, bass, drums, and vocals, nor the new electronic sound that today is erasing even minimal national distinctions in pop, which in the not-so-distant Golden Age of Rock still resisted corporate homogenization.

The language of architecture, of course, employs the universal grammar of columns, façades, and balustrades. Thus, architectural style is immediately accessible to viewers, even at the most elementary level, whether they have sharpened their eye for spatial creativity on the wondrous exuberance of Antonio Gaudí, the Secessionist monumentality of Miklós Ybl, or the geometric boldness of Frank Lloyd Wright. The architectural imagination might daydream about façades without ornament, might renounce palisades or bracket the ever-useful idiom of arches and portals, but whatever sort of architecture it produces, it will, in some essential way, still be recognizable.

For literature, alas, the situation is quite different. Indeed, it is ontologically different. Literature is unique among the arts insofar as its sole medium, language, is unique. Through language, the individual self is subtly linked to the spiritual and material achievements of the national cultural totality. Unlike nonverbal theater, which with a wave of the hand can dismiss the script, literature cannot do away with language. A writer cannot reject language, even though he or she may be well aware that, as Roland Barthes asserted, "language is the worst of all possible conventions." Performers in contemporary nonverbal theater can flee the stifling linearity of the text, seeking salvation in the apparently free language of the body. But writers? We hit a brick wall: the persistent corporeality of language. Even when authors such as Antonin Artaud, Georges Bataille, and Pier Paolo Pasolini strove to convey in profoundly personal terms the immediate physicality of blood, semen, and snot, they still had to deal with letters, words, and writing. Literature is anchored in received models of collective experience and linguistic representation, regardless of the extent to which these representations are challenged.

What I am saying may disgust liberal pseudo-cosmopolitans, who, when they hear words like "identity," "nation," and "collective," start mindlessly parroting Gertrude Stein's enigmatic dictum about Oakland: "There is no there

there." Afraid that they might fall prey to accusations of nationalism, these pseudo-cosmopolitans would rather sweep national identity quietly under the carpet. But anational liberal mercantilism, as it manifests itself in much of post-communist Central and Eastern Europe, cleverly mimicking the Marxist-inspired rejection of the national question, is little more than a mirror image of popular nationalism. The one feigns an indifference toward nationality that easily turns into a prostration before all things Western, while the other barks viciously at anything "foreign," "alien," or "different." Both fail to articulate a political vision that sees membership in a distinct ethnic collective neither as a privilege to be flaunted nor as a disgrace to be concealed.

Well, even if it is something disgraceful, I cannot keep quiet. Personal experience, poetic intuition, and rational reflection all persuade me that, even if a literary work can be adequately described in terms of international styles (*nouveau roman*, literature of the absurd, dirty realism, minimalism, postmodernism, and so on), it can be fully assimilated only within a national cultural identity and the tradition it supports. Consequently, because they have to break through the barricade of national language, literary works face a much more difficult, much longer road to international recognition than do other artistic disciplines. It is no surprise, then—although it continues to be disheartening—that on the American cultural horizon the Slovene literary imagination has no basic reference points.

Such reference points would include literary histories, Slovene participation in literary and cultural journals, surveys of the development of national identity, memoiristic writings, and journalistic travelogues through Slovene geography and culture. Completely forgotten today, for example, are the novels and essays of Louis Adamic (1899–1951), a Slovene native who came to the New World as a boy. Although he exchanged his mother tongue for English, his writings reveal that he recalled the country of his early childhood with affection. Between the two world wars, he wrote several widely read and critically acclaimed prose works in a social realist vein along the lines of Upton Sinclair and Theodore Dreiser. *The Native's Return* (1934) and *Struggle* (1934) are among his most successful works.

Nor have Slovene émigré writers ever been represented in anthologies of American non-English writing. In 2000, Marc Shell and Werner Sollors compiled *The Multilingual Anthology of American Literature: A Reader of Original Texts with English Translations*, revealing America's unique and for the most part neglected diversity of literary traditions. But no Slovenes were included. Shell and Sollors's anthology would have provided, for example, an excellent opportunity to publish Ludve Potokar's *The Guilty Source* [Krivi vir], an unfinished novel that is nevertheless emotionally stirring. Potokar, who after fleeing communist Slovenia in 1945 could not embrace any of the competing anti-communist ideologies, was scorned by the Slovene émigré circles of both North and South America. Woefully isolated, he lived and wrote, in his mother tongue, on the very fringes of the Slovene community in Cleveland and finally died in the Canadian wilderness, a despairing, disillusioned, and twice-ignored writer. Such examples serve to make the simple point that there are precious few experts in Eastern European literature who can place the fruits of Slovene creative mind in a recognizable frame of reference.

The End of Arcadia

As I stood in St. Mark's Bookstore paging through *The Selected Poems of Tomaž Šalamun*, I tried not to think about the sad fact of Slovenia's literary absence. This was not just a question of wounded pride; above all, it showed that the Slovene national identity lacked its own visible place among the multitude of contemporary identities. I was trying not to think about the fact that no one else could share my distress. No one from among the American poets, students, professors, journalists, intellectuals, and other managers of symbols and ideas, who on television and radio, in films, newspapers, and college classrooms help determine how people perceive the cultural tracks made by individuals and nations in the quicksand of modern times—not one of these men and women, any of whom could have been standing next to me leafing through other books, could share the painful dialectic of rejection and love that I felt in my conflicted attitude toward national identity.

A sense of affiliation toward one's own "imagined community" is particularly strong among poets from nations with a history of subjugation. The Irish poet Seamus Heaney, in an interview with David Montenegro, noted that the dominant themes in Irish poetry today are spiritual displacement and a profound lack of confidence in the stability of the world. In his opinion, the metaphors of doubt in the metaphysical order that underpin contemporary Irish poetry derive primarily from the fact that throughout his nation's history there has been an ongoing interchange among the forces of endless conflict, violent rebellion, and grievous loss. Heaney speaks about W. H. Auden as a giant of English literature but confesses that Auden's literary range is not entirely accessible to him. Although at first glance this statement may seem surprising, Heaney offers a convincing explanation. He points to Auden's unmistakable desire to construct a panegyric to domesticity, the kind of thing canonical English poetry can celebrate only because it is embedded in history that is not thoroughly negative—a history that is not one of destruction, grief, and defeat. Contemporary Irish poetry, although written mostly in English, carries within itself the painful memory of the primary collective, reverberating with the abuses of colonialism, the terror of the potato famine, the imposed division of the country, and the humiliation of marginality. Heaney's aesthetic vision, in comparison with Auden's, thus possesses essentially different and darker accents. The two poets might share in the use of the linguistic forms, but they do not share the same historical experience or the same collective tradition.

> At the time, of course, I wasn't thinking about this. I thought nothing about this at the time. I did my practical criticism and ignored all the contexts. Then in my thirties and forties I became aware, if you like, of poems not just as cher-

ishable and delightful linguistic events, but as symptoms and conduits of history and culture, and all that. . . . They are the symptoms and passages of culture and history. (182)

Heaney is here referring to the importance of historical—that is, collective—existence for the iconography and symbolism of poetic speech.

But the Slovene collective existence is more or less unknown internationally. This fact hit home in the summer of 1991, after Slovenia's Ten-Day War for independence, when I was accompanying a foreign cultural journalist on his travels through the country.

Post-communist Slovenia is gradually, and somewhat bashfully, opening itself to the wide world. Each year, especially in summer, it receives more visitors: inquisitive Western journalists, adventurous students, businessmen, and international con artists. Slovene émigrés also return. Their children enroll in summer language classes and, in their Australian, Latin American, or German accents, struggle to speak the language of their parents or grandparents. Small and homogenous, Slovenia will probably never become a Tower of Babel, but in the summer a bewitching yet unassuming concert of foreign tongues nevertheless echoes off the walls of the recently renovated mansions that hug the river banks beneath Ljubljana Castle. This testifies to an interest in novelty, the kind of attention foreigners pay a country that appeared so suddenly, with its newly won sovereignty, on the maps of Europe.

As I travel with some of these foreigners around Slovenia, I often notice that things self-evident to me appear bewildering to them. For several years now, I have been explaining the peculiarities of Slovene culture not only to my American wife but also to numerous writers visiting from abroad. And at least one of them, Christopher Merrill, in *Only the Nails Remain: Scenes from the Balkan War,* apparently found some of my attempts at explanation valuable.

Still, I am somewhat disturbed by how provisional my accounts can be, and many facets of the communal life remain impervious to reason. A woman's seductive gesture and downturned eyes in a courtyard in the Mediterranean town of Piran; the collective Slovene fear of drafts; the way an extended elbow protects a glass as it is raised to the lips; the crowds of pilgrims at the Savica Waterfall in the Alps, where, according to an epic poem by the Romantic poet France Prešeren, a Slovene pagan leader accepted Christianity (the first of many conversions in the name of the collective survival)—in the barefoot anthropology of foreign visitors all these things represent a kind of encrypted mental code that might just elucidate the hidden nature of this unusually small yet persevering "tribe."

These shared trips proved to be a most interesting cultural experiment. They were itineraries of both pride and guilt, outlining the peculiar nature of contemporary Slovenian reality, where remnants of the old communist regime were crossbred with the achievements of the emerging democratic order. I had mistakenly thought I knew this country simply because I lived within its borders. It was thus a sobering experience to accompany foreign visitors on their travels, for I was forced to explain the history and customs of the various regions we visited. I soon learned just how difficult it is to explain in concise, clear, and simple terms such things as the different politicized views on Slovene ethnogenesis, the faded glory of the seventh-century independent state of Carantania, the religious grip of of the medieval Roman Catholic archdiocese of Aquileia, and the unquestioned Slovene identification with Alpine farming culture. Eventually, in 1999, I attempted to provide a literary map of my country in "Slovenia: A Brief Literary History," largely as a response to my frustrations with curious visitors and their lack of information. It was essential to fill the void; otherwise, it would get filled with the kind of condescending clichés that fast-track journalists frequently mouth.

I remember one journalist particularly well. He stood there, eyes wide open, out of breath after our brisk descent from the Renaissance castle in the town of Ptuj, about to step into a pub with a chrome-plated bar. The dust on the visor of his baseball cap had barely settled as he turned it around in a kind of studiously casual gesture so that the late summer sun shone on his bronzed face—a face that had seen Sudan, Ukraine, and Nepal. He was one of those visitors who get so inspired by beautiful landscapes, captivating small towns, sophisticated city life, and the easy-going local population that when they return home they write a laudatory article about it all for the travel section of their newspaper. Now he was content simply to deliver a bit of sincere, well-meaning praise: "Stay just as you are," he said, "hidden beneath the Alps, and don't let anyone know you're here!

This is just a benign variation on that terribly persistent trope of the nameless bucolic realm where people live in fecund contact with nature, protected from the harmful effects of the West's high-tech civilization. This paradigm attracts nostalgic leftists, who for the most part still feed on the mistaken concept of "nations outside of history." In a misguided flight from the alienated society of the postmodern West, they take refuge, possibly against their own inclinations, in an ideology of "blood and soil." The Austrian writer Peter Handke, in a provocative critique of Slovenian independence entitled "A Dreamer's Farewell to the New Country: Memories of Slovenia" (1991), was perhaps the first to propound this paradigm explicitly in relation to Slovenia. I do not think I am being overly pessimistic if I say that this kind of obnoxiously patronizing attitude will probably shape the Western perception of my country for a long time to come."

.

America, Aversion, Attraction

No wonder, then, that I tried to block out any thought about Slovene cultural anonymity as I leafed through Šalamun's translated poems. I wanted to forget that no one else in St. Mark's Bookstore shared my thoughts about Josip Murn's "poplar all alone" or about the significance of the Slovene national myth of Beautiful Vida, who longs for unseen lands but then gets homesick when she travels abroad. No one else could join me in lamenting the fact that by the time the first Slovene novel was written, French realist novels were already ensconced in the textbooks. Nor could anyone share my lyric inclinations, which oscillated between Srečko Kosovel's apocalyptic premonitions and Edvard Kocbek's estatic oneness with the great chain of being. In Slovenia, I could share these dilemmas, sorrows, and enthusiasms in literary discussions with my fellow poets, but on the American side of the Atlantic no one would have the faintest idea what I was talking about. In America, the world of Slovene literature was a total *terra incognita*. It is not surprising, then, that the idea of America fills Slovene writers with both aversion and attraction.

Drago Jančar's novel *Mocking Desire* provides an excellent example of the Slovene response to America. Specifically, it delineates the disappointed repulsion that arises from the gap between the mythic image of America and its unforgiving reality. On the one hand, there is the ideal of individual freedom; on the other, America's brutal work ethic, the regulation of pleasure, and professionalized fantasy-mongering. With great aesthetic flair, Jančar's novel exposes the burden of anonymity, as his hero experiences it in the humid decadence of New Orleans: he sits in a bar where none of the regulars have the slightest inkling that this melancholy drinker is, somewhere on the other side of the planet, being toasted as a playwright whose new piece has just opened at the Slovene National Theater.

The novel's hero eventually does shed his Central European awkwardness but no more than is necessary for him to surrender to the unforeseen charms of the American life. In the midst of carnal pleasure and clairvoyant meditations, he slowly comes to understand that his proper place is, despite its spatial limitations and spiritual confinement, at home in Slovenia. He sees his homeland more clearly now that he has confronted something different and other. He realizes that his place lies in the world of small towns, which, though dominated by petty and resentful elites, are also permeated with a troubled history that not only inspires and paralyzes him, but also morally binds him—precisely because it does set limits and so strengthens his sense of community. He learns once more that his home is amid the rustling ancient forests of the Pohorje Massif, where hidden Celtic burial mounds suggest an existential bond to the resilient collective memory, which acquires its full meaning only now that he has completed his adventure in a land obsessed with the rituals of an eternal "now."

My own American experience was somewhat different from that of Jančar's protagonist. I was not disheartened by the anonymity I saw as a constituent part of American life, although I would be lying if I said it did not disturb me. I felt it as a kind of compulsory tax one pays during a necessary period of adjustment. At the same time, I was trying to shape a different story for myself, a different "narrative frame," such as we all spontaneously create in order to comprehend the events of everyday life. From my very first visit to America, I saw this inevitable anonymity as an irresistable challenge, one that dared you to show what you can do and prove your worth.

Perhaps this is why I examined Šalamun's book with such respectful admiration. But there were other reasons, too, why it commanded my attention. For one thing, Šalamun was the only living Slovene writer who had seen his book published in United States—no small achievement in the highly competitive world of American literary publishing. For another, I knew the author person-ally—had known him ever since my college days in the early 1980s, when we were drawn together not only by the conspiracy of poetic discourse and battles with the political authorities, but, above all, by bonds of friendship. Developing over time, our friendship taught me the "courage of being," as theologian Paul Tillich termed the existential imperative to be one's self. Šalamun did not teach me how to write—indeed, I may be the only Slovene poet of my generation whose literary formation was not influenced by his poetry—but how to move through the social and cultural space, how to make a foreign country one's tem-porary home, and how to understand the symbolic worlds of foreign places. Šalamun's example undoubtedly saved me a decade of trial and error. Once, when I was a restless young student, he even stopped me from joining the French Foreign Legion (as I now see it, I had succumbed to a romantic infatua-tion with the great authority of evil).

It was Šalamun who taught me just how sterile, if not patently dangerous, the Slovene dualism about foreign lands could be. Slovenes either swoon un-critically over Western books and ideas, or smugly, and no less uncritically, proclaim their own self-involvement. Both camps display the vulgar philosophy of social climbers, the mentality of a small town that is no longer a village but is hardly an urban center, either. Giving themselves pseudo-cosmopolitan airs, they see the international flow of ideas not as a symbolic exchange of gifts, but rather as a great marketplace in which there are no producers, only consumers. They understand the international circulation of ideas as a treasure house where they can passively satisfy their own whims, but they lack the self-confidence to enrich or expand it with their own vision. Šalamun, however, with his trenchant understanding of the writing life and his patrician approach toward unique exis-tential experience as something that should yield a unique lyric vision, helped me overcome the inferiority complex of a poet from an unknown tradition. In other words, he encouraged me to see that the crucial thing is not the size or importance of the nation that speaks the language you write in, but rather the genuine cosmos of the poetry you create, dictated by both god and demon.

The National Torso

When, ten years after my initial visit to St. Mark's Bookstore, I stood behind the podium of the New York's Academy of American Poets, which only rarely in-vites non-American poets to read their work, I was filled with a bathetic sense of pride. Šalamun, my loyal advocate and, at the same time, the only reference point I had as I sailed the waters of American and international poetic life—had never stood on this stage. With trembling hands and a dry mouth, I was about to read from my first book of poems published in English, *Anxious Moments* (1994), which fellow poet Christopher Merrill and I had translated together. My stage fright was somewhat lessened not only because I had just returned from a short, but intense reading tour of American universities; I now felt a certain paradoxical self-confidence that had been completely unknown to me a decade earlier, when I was gloomily paging through Šalamun's book. Without any referential frame, recognizable tradition, or great literary predecessors that might have helped anchor my writing in the minds of my American audience, without anything that might situate my prose poems in a larger cultural context, I had arrived at this significant public appearance in a country where most of the population had not even heard the name of my homeland, let alone knew how to spell it.

First, there was the obligatory introduction, in which the Kashmiri American poet and critic Aga Shahid Ali described my poetic practice in a short burst of enthusiasm, then sketched out a few basic parameters of Slovene culture—sixteenth-century Protestantism, the translation of the Bible, the reassertion of Roman Catholicism, the Partisans and the liberation struggle, the communist regime. Then five hundred pairs of eyes were gazing at me. I recited one of my poems, first in Slovene, then in my well-rehearsed English. At that moment, perhaps more than ever before, I experienced a sobering dénouement that forced me to face facts. Suddenly, it dawned on me that Šalamun had been right when he once bitterly remarked that the Slovene people represent a kind of "national torso," lacking head and upper arms, an incomplete nation.

The Serbian American poet Charles Simic, who had kindly written the preface to my *Anxious Moments,* read after me. The recipient of many enviable honors, including the Pulitzer Prize and the MacArthur "Genius" grant, Simic needed no introduction. Nor did his poetic practice require any special explanation, since his work enjoyed a triple framing. One of the main sources of Simic's poetry, besides French surrealism and American imagism, is found in Serbian folklore, the national myths and primordial cosmology of Simic's birthplace. European literary Romantics, particularly Goethe, had been fairly enamored with this ethnic heritage.

But the Slovene tradition, and I with it, needed the assistance of a friendly guide in order to be presentable. A dark, sobering rain began to fall in the pond of my self-confidence, forcing me to see, in the lack of a Slovene presence on America's cultural map, a blank spot, the sort of unknown region that medieval cartographers evocatively labeled *ubi leones*—"where lions are"—unexplored territory where no surveyor had set foot. This lack of a recognizable cultural and literary context, had motivated Šalamun to undertake, with his grand mythologizing talent, the project of inventing his own, personal, idiosyncratic tradition. In his poems, as well as in press interviews, Šalamun has indeed managed to create a venerable personal cosmology, complete with illustrious, possibly Jewish ancestors, apocryphal heraldry, cosmopolitan geography, tumultuous history, esoteric symbols, and loved ones—an entire panoply of all the people, animals, and things he ever touched as a poet, weaving them all into an unending stream of lyrical documents. In certain rare cases, with the best literary artists, the fateful primacy of the mother tongue is diluted, and its pressure migrates to the margins of creative interest.

But even for Šalamun, this bold attempt did not entirely succeed, although of all Slovene writers he has come closest. But I am convinced that, had there been Western translations of the aesthetic and conceptual works that shaped the start of his career—the works of the Slovene avant-garde movements of the 1960s—then Šalamun's innovative contribution to international poetry would have found a place in the standard literary encyclopedias. To explain what I mean, I will need to make a brief digression.

Slovenia's Language Poetry

Experimental flights of fancy, a necessary linguistic arrogance, a fervent assault on teary-eyed humanism, the rejection of transcendent order and rebellion against the rules of grammar and syntax, the separation of things from words, the radical emancipation of the linguistic material—these are only a few of the distinguishing features that comparative literature graduate students all over the world use to describe the semiotics of the American school of poetry known as "L=A=N=G=U=A=G=E." Born in the 1970s in the bohemian cafés of San Francisco, it followed in the noble tradition of *épate le bourgeois*, causing a commotion in American literary journals and thumbing its nose at the guardians of academia. Today, however, its leading proponents, such as the poet Charles Bernstein, are literary stars with chairs at prestigious universities, where they watch over the now perhaps waning movement that once breathed fresh air into America's literary life.

But if you turned your gaze toward Slovenia, you might be surprised to learn that an almost identical literary movement, known as "reism," emerged there a full decade earlier. Tomaž Šalamun, Franci Zagoričnik, Iztok Geister-Plamen, Tomaž Kralj, Andrej Medved, and Matjaž Hanžek, as well as many other poets who cut their teeth in the 1960s, were rebelling against the same sentimental humanism that existentialist poets such as Dane Zajc, Veno Taufer, and Gregor Strniša had already rejected. But a new movement was needed to put a decisive end to the remaining expressive norms. These neo-avant-garde poets took it on themselves to finish off the last vestiges of traditional literature. The trends that emerged with this new poetics—"reism" (focusing solely on things), "carnism" (focusing on the excesses of the body), and "ludism," (focusing on trans-rational playfulness)—changed Slovene poetry for all time.

The neo-avant-garde poets, led by Šalamun, concentrated on the inherent potential of language—"linguism" was yet another apt label these poets used, describing an emphasis on an indeterminable linguistic drive—and thus demonstrated that they were not simply following international trends but, in their most visionary works, anticipating them. Šalamun, by the way, made the first of his many extended travels to the United States at the beginning of the 1970s—when Slovene reism was already in full swing—and befriended some of the L=A=N=G=U=A=G=E poets, including Bob Perelman. The Slovene poet can, in fact, be considered an international L=A=N=G=U=A=G=E poet *avant la lettre.*

Had the creative imagination of Šalamun and his Slovene colleagues been translated right away into the "major" languages, and thus become known to international or, at least, American literary circles, then the wind of literary fashion might have blown the other way. Frederic Jameson, one of the most prolific gurus of Marxist cultural criticism, in his highly influential and fre-quently quoted 1984 book *Postmodernism, or, The Cultural Logic of Late Capitalism,* analyzed the typical semantic and morphological features of a poem by Perelman, discovering in its texture the universal imprint of nascent post-modernism. In doing so, he drew the attention of the international reading public to Perelman's poetry. For reasons of textual innovation alone he could have done the same thing with one of Šalamun's poems. But Jameson could have done this, at least in theory, only if he had known of Šalamun's poetry in the first place. Any poem Jameson chose would have had to be accessible as a com-plete poetic and historical-cultural phenomenon, that is, not only as an isolated poem, but also as a constitutive part of a larger artistic movement. It would have had to function within an obligatory collective context. Slovene reism, which nowadays lies buried in local literary archives, might, then, have contributed its part, along with American L=A=N=G=U=A=G=E poetry, to the worldwide neo-avant-garde explosion at a time when it was still possible to appreciate dra-matic challenges to artistic taboos. These kinds of challenges, however, lost their radical edge once postmodern babbling became a main staple of the cul-tural diet, in which, to be sure, "anything goes" but precious little is existentially compelling or aesthetically exciting.

Measuring Up to American Standards

Without stories, life becomes dull. Without poetic longing, a person becomes stupid. The *mythos,* or story, of the existential human drama is always a deter-mining lever, triggering our dreams, indignation, and compassion. Ultimately, our encounter with the stories of art and literature makes possible a much clearer view into our own story, our own fate. Art, which depicts the mysterious forces that shape or wreck our lives, cannot be easily rejected, for without its magic, writers would have to concede that the lifelong commitment to recording hope and fear becomes little more than an amusing whim. This awareness, in fact, is what keeps an ancient sense of *mythos* alive in our confused hearts. Under the writer's skillful pen, a story about an individual grows into a story about society and the heavy problems of the world, which readers experience just as the liter-ary protagonist does, with the same sorrows and the same affections.

The childhood of humanity was very familiar with the inescapable connec-tion between individual destiny and the destiny of the larger community. In an-tiquity, it was an essential principle of rhetoric that "the story talks about you"— *de te fabula narratur.* Slovene writers should be able to hope that, as their books are translated and published in America, their personal stories, and the collective Slovene story, will speak to people throughout the world. Getting something published in America not only stakes a claim in world's largest literary market, it also makes you, in principle, accessible to anyone who reads in English, the modern *lingua franca*—to many more people, that is, than just native English speakers. Thanks to the activities of academic and small presses, as well as contemporary American translations of works by Polish, Czech, Lithuanian, Hungarian, and Romanian writers, I can, to a certain degree, keep abreast of these interesting literatures—and so can many others—without having to command a knowledge of a half a dozen East European languages. This dialectic of individual/universal feeds my stubborn conviction that the best Slovene writers can—and absolutely must—transcend the barriers that now exist thanks to a dearth of translated Slovene literature.

Life in America is, of course, faster-paced, more stressful, and more demanding than in Slovenia, and consequently, the existential "wear and tear" is greater. But at the same time, as an important counterbalance, the social, intellectual, and cultural advantages are also greater. In particular, the large metropolitan areas—New York, San Francisco, Los Angeles, Boston, Chicago—offer an unending parade of the world's most extravagant and accomplished talent, with concerts, readings, books, films, operas, exhibitions, theater, and so on. All this flurry is stimulating, but it can also be a burden. The writer who ventures onto the American literary scene is forced to compete not only with American writers, but with the best and the brightest on the planet. Indeed, at least since World War II, America's cultural importance has transcended any single tradition; it has become a stage for the entire world and so has enjoyed enormous international attention.

Thanks to all the cultural activity that takes place in America, standards are higher there. This does not mean people are automatically better writers. But they have access to a far more extensive artistic and cultural life, with numerous publishing houses, magazines and journals, anthologies, critics, prizes and awards. All this swirl creates a much fiercer, more heightened competition among writers, which, in turn, triggers a continuous demand for more rigorous standards. What with the mega-merges of publishing houses that are, since the new Gilded Age of the 1990s, becoming little more than divisions of corporate entertainment conglomerates, these rigorous standards may, however, apply only to the ever shrinking field of serious fiction, essays, and poetry.

Still, editors and writers are always keeping a close eye on competitors, eagerly looking for the right moment to advance. This is the reason for such an obsessive concentration on local American events, at least in mainstream cultural production. As far as literature, and especially poetry, is concerned, poets do not usually get their first book published until they are in their late twenties; their lyric voice must first be thoroughly tested in literary journals and magazines. The competition is just too strong to permit overnight sensations. This mechanism has its advantages; for one thing, it maintains aesthetic competence. But the downside is that the greater part of the literary publishing machinery cannot recognize a truly original voice, one that differs in profound ways from established standards of excellence.

John Ashbery, whom many consider America's greatest living poet, is the rare exception to this rule; his early success made him something of a *Wunderkind*. But a poet's rise is usually gradual and slow, with individual poetic practice being constantly measured against other poetic voices and critical response. At the same time, every new poetic work must be read against a huge mass of books both past and present. Clearly, the sifting process is extremely arduous and time-consuming.

Those Europeans who have little real knowledge of the diverse forms of American cultural production are usually the loudest to belittle it, grinding out hackneyed complaints about how literature in the United States has become nothing more than a "commodity" that is "superficial" and "celebrity-driven." Such phrases are, I suspect, understandable attempts to conceal Europe's fear of self-examination as it increasingly defines itself in an opposition to the United States (even more so after the George W. Bush adminstration issued a licence for state violence in the open-ended "war on terror"). It is true (and so obvious it is hardly worth mentioning) that, as far as instant best sellers go, the aesthetic product is seen purely as merchandise. But the most interesting thing about America—and something rather hard to discern from a distance—is the vast number of small literary and critical quarterlies, as well as academic and small-press publishers, that make room for various kinds of experimental writing. At the same time, American intellectual and artistic elites, supported by philanthropic institutions and nurtured by competitive graduate schools, help create a sophisticated, if sometimes affectatious urban mentality. It was this mentality that once inspired Danilo Kiš—to my mind, the greatest Yugoslav writer of the twentieth century and a European master par excellence—to exclaim that he would move from Paris to New York in a minute if only his English were better.

Far from feeling discouraged by the American literary scene, I wanted to see myself reflected in that sophisticated mentality. I wanted to test the aesthetic power and existential currency of my own poetic practice and explore the possible range of the Slovene lyric tradition. I wanted to break through the conspiracy of indifference that engulfs anyone who writes in a "small" language and, at the same time, refute, at least to some degree, the self-fulfilling prophecy about the defensive nature of Slovene literary life. After all—to use an analogy that seems rather appropriate, given the inspirational proximity of poetry and wine—you cannot even dream of being a great wine connoisseur if the only taste your palate knows, comes from the grapes in your neighbour's vineyard. Such challenges transformed my initial desperation into euphoria. Then, after several years of living in New York and having a fair number of my poems appear in American literary magazines, I was suddenly possesed by a demented idea. I decided to publish an anthology of contemporary Slovene poetry. I suppose I wanted to see if Slovene poetry could stand on its own two feet, independent and unaided. For only thus would it be able to tell its own story—one that might, somehow, find an American and international readership.

A Piece in the International Mosaic

Little did I know how frustrating this task would be. I could work on it only in my spare time—at first, only in the evenings until I completed the course work for my doctoral studies. I did not imagine the difficulties involved with just assembling the basic material. Only a very limited selection of contemporary Slovene poetry in the original was available at the New York Public Library and Columbia University. But once I had embarked on my descent into the inferno of amateur editorship, I stubbornly refused to give up. I spent countless hours in patient discussions with the two or three American translators competent enough to to work with Slovene. I despaired over the Slovene obsession with the demanding "pathology of the sonnet" (a form I, too, work in), for it is nearly impossible to translate sonnets adequately. I wrote appeals for financial support and nervously waited for replies. On the rare occasions when I met Slovene businessmen in New York, I tried to appeal to their latent generosity, and so managed to collect several hundred dollars to cover the all-important start-up capital. I combed manuscripts, assembled and edited hastily translated poems, suggested corrections, spent hours on the telephone and in front of the computer screen, and wrote pleading letters, all from a dingy little studio apartment in the East Village.

In brief fits of laughable grandiosity, I dubbed my place—complete with a hot plate sitting on the corner of the desk that did double duty as both kitchen and library—the Command Tower of Slovene Literary Promotion. From here, day after day, I would set out on expeditions into the pulsating heart of the city. At poetry readings and literary soirées, at quick midday coffees and in the drunken haze of late-night parties below Fourteenth Street hosted by small-press editors and literary enthusiasts, I searched for a possible publisher for "my" anthology. I wanted this book to be the first stone in an international mosaic, to help create the frame of reference I had so dearly lacked when I first arrived in America.

With the resigned realism of an editor aware of both his own limitations and those of the literary tradition he wanted to present, I knew I would not be able to get any of the big-name publishing houses excited about my project. It could hardly have been otherwise, for what was out there already? None of the established literary journals had ever devoted an entire issue to Slovene poetry; only a few handfuls of poems had appeared in three or four journals. Richard Jackson, a poet and professor at the University of Tennessee at Chattanooga and a frequent visitor to Slovenia, had begun publishing as a labor of love the Poetry Miscellany Chapbooks, a series of modest but informative booklets, with negligible print runs, devoted to individual Slovene poets. Ecco Press had published the selection of Šalamun's work. And a few scattered Slovene poems had appeared in anthologies of East European poetry, from publishers like Penguin and MacMillan. And that was it. Small wonder, then, that I did not even attempt to approach such venerable publishing houses as Random House, Simon and Schuster, or Farrar, Strauss and Giroux. It would have been a waste of time.

My daily rummaging through the nooks and crannies of the literary world, guest-lecturing at universities, zealous exhortations, carefully composed requests, and impassioned pleading finally did bear fruit. Thanks to the mediation of translator Sonja Kravanja, and to my own extended visit to the far southwestern corner of the United States, a micro-press publisher in Santa Fe, New Mexico, warmed to my insane idea. *Prisoners of Freedom: Contemporary Slovenian Poetry* was finally published in 1993 by Pedernal Press in a series that already included anthologies of French and Korean poetry, as well as international experimental work.

After two years of arduous negotiations, meticulous galley-proof corrections, disputes with the printer, and proofreader interpolations, I went to the post office at Penn Station to pick up a package containing ten copies of the anthology. My heart was racing like that of a pimply-faced teenager on his first date. I anxiously ripped open the greasy wrapping with my apartment key. The sight of these books, their covers decorated with a frail green angel, was proof that I was not dreaming. At last! I held in my hands the first American publication of an anthology of contemporary Slovene poetry—the first anthology in which Slovene poets did not have to crowd under the bell-jar of Eastern Europe or Yugoslavia, the first anthology in which Slovene poets stood alone, without excuses or mitigating circumstances. How could I fuss about the fact that the Slovene letters *č, ž,* and *š*—a nightmare for American printers—were all in italics, with diacritical marks that sometimes overlapped adjacent letters? How could I quibble over the fact that the designer had rushed the job, and the type on the opposing pages was not properly aligned? This was hardly the time to worry about the two names missing from the table of contents or to fret over the book's modest distribution. For with this anthology, whatever it might lack in design or content, the Slovene lyric tradition could join other national poetry anthologies in the bookstores and libraries of America.

Even such intellectual giants as Jacques Derrida, Julia Kristeva, and Jean Baudrillard first had to come to this country and have their works appear in American translations before they could become international names in philosophy. Without a book published in America, very few literary or critical writers can hope to win extensive international acclaim in a world defined, for better or for worse, by the *Pax Americana,* the constant humming of the intellectual mill of American universities and college markets, the demands and whims of the American book trade, and the overwhelming influence of American mass culture.

As I write these lines, my mind staggers under the weight of the complex processes that today bind together Slovene and international cultural life. And then I think of the late Slovene writer Marjan Rožanc. His effort to penetrate the meaning of existence in a world without meaning has strongly influenced the contemporary Slovene essay, particularly in the way he used personal experience to bolster universal speculation. Rožanc's excellent essay, "The Neoplatonic Cosmos," provides a good example of this.

Beginning with recollections of his old farmhouse in a village in Slovenia's rocky Karst region above the Adriatic Sea, Rožanc fleshed out a longing for the wide open spaces that Mediterranean civilization invites. At the same time, he showed in just a few paragraphs how the search for a home—a place where sky and land meet in absolute truth—is driven by a deep human need to be linked to the larger community, where emotional, historical, and metaphysical bonds sustain both head and heart.

But Rožanc was much too subtle an essayist to be content with some pastoral idyll; instead, he exploded the kind of illusion entertained by those who reject anything unknown, foreign, or different, anything that lies outside the well-worn arsenal of nationalist rhetoric. Rather, he suggested that our authentic dwelling-place, if it is to be spiritually free, must be found in a paradoxical but existentially necessary oscillation between home and foreign lands. In a single short sentence, he cogently summarized his creative and personal endeavor: "I had to tear myself away from the world of my home in order to feel that I was at home." That's it: to take a step back, like an impressionist painter who perceives the whole meaning of the shimmering dabs of color on the canvas only when he sees them from a critical distance—up close they seem a chaotic jumble. We can properly judge the possibilities and obstacles of our national cultural experience only when we view it from afar. If Slovene poets and writers let ourselves be guided by this principle, it will be hard to get lost on the sea of the unknown. In the lands beyond the Alps we will make our way slowly but confidently, without any sense of inferiority but unhampered, too, by vanity, forging a path for those who follow. Literature is, after all, a long-distance race.

Rožanc's cosmopolitan view and Šalamun's aesthetic originality may serve as guideposts, giving us reason to hope that one day the Slovene literary tradition—and its "imagined community"—will no longer be a dreary *terra incognita*, but will instead hold a legitimate place in the international cultural mosaic. When the cumulative Slovene creative tradition is no longer merely material for obtuse hair-splitting among Slavists, when it can be seen as a flexible vital bond with the past, where the seeds of the future lie dormant—then the most daring writers will perhaps see something besides their own anxieties in the opening lines of Šalamun's poem "My First Time in New York City" (from the 1976 book *Celebration* [Praznik]): "My first time in New York City / I was scared shitless."

Then Slovene poets will not be petrified by the fearful asymmetry they encounter in the world beyond their familiar homeland. Instead they will find inspiration there for great ambitions, exploding the dictum about the borders of one's language being the borders of one's world, and they will take sustenance in the notion that the individual lyric vision can convey a universal message. No need to look far for such inspiration. The conclusion of Šalamun's poem reveals a conviction that the rhythms of the world's artistic constellations transcend the limitations of nationality. Representing both Šalamun's aesthetic program and an existential account of an artist's destiny, the poem ends prophetically, in self-assurance and in mystic ecstasy:

. . .
and I
suddenly
saw
with perfect
clarity,
that it was only a matter of time before
New York City would vomit me forth
into the sky
like a star.

(Translated by Michael Biggins)

Chapter 3

The Cosmopolitan Spirit under Siege

The Uses of National Stereotypes

The train was carrying us slowly toward Trieste. From Ljubljana, it takes only two hours to reach this Italian city at the northern end of the Adriatic Sea. Once the principal port of Austria-Hungary, Trieste used to be a cosmopolitan place, home to people from many of the empire's diverse ethnic and religious communities. With the collapse of the Austro-Hungarian Empire and the remapping of Europe after World War I, Trieste came under Italian control. Some thirty years later, when the city became a pawn in the Cold War power-play that followed World War II, its multiethnic character was a critical factor in the decision to establish the Free Territory of Trieste as a United Nations protectorate. Under the joint administration of the United States, Britain, and Yugoslavia, festering ethnic rivalries between Italians and Slavs were further aggravated by ideology as the capitalist West and the communist East vied for the spoils of war. When the border was finally settled in 1954, the ethnic Slovene territory, the city's hinterland, became part of Yugoslavia, while the city of Trieste itself was given to Italy. No longer an important port, the city gradually fell into state-pampered obscurity as an Italian cul-de-sac.

For Yugoslavs, however, and especially for Slovenes, whose Socialist Republic bordered on Italy, Trieste soon became important for new reasons. In the minds of several generations, the city appeared as a glittering, seductive place, burgeoning with stores and shops that offered treasures unavailable at home. Trieste was the mythical embodiment of the West. Crossborder smuggling came in both wholesale and retail varieties, as black-market networks facilitated the transfer of people and finances, while ordinary families made regular excursions to the city in pursuit of consumerist fantasies. A special kind of hunger was sated in Trieste, a hunger for Fiat spare parts, nifty deodorant sticks, goose-down sleeping bags, fragrant espresso coffee, trendy Levi's jeans, and other necessities that could not be purchased in Ljubljana.

But Trieste has still another significance for Slovenes. As we approached the city by train, I explained to my wife, Erica, that Trieste was the place where, in the period between the two world wars, Italian Fascists burned down the Slovene Cultural Center and that even today the Triestine Slovene minority lacks certain basic rights as an ethnic group. Erica, an American who, understandably, does not possess a detailed knowledge of Slovene history, listened to what I had to say and then, with typical Anglo-Saxon common sense, observed wryly, "You Slovenes see Trieste only in extremes: it's either a hotbed of Fascism or a great big shopping mall."

I was stopped in my cliché-ridden tracks. What she said was true. Trieste, after all, is much more than just a chapter of Slovene history, albeit one shot through with misery and oppression. As the train snaked down the slopes from the Karst plateau, my nostrils widened slightly to catch the scent of the sea-washed breeze over the cliffs above the Adriatic. For a brief moment, the white tower of the Thurn-und-Taxis castle flashed in the distance, and I imagined the slender figure of Rainer Maria Rilke, who in 1912 wrote the first two of his immortal *Duino Elegies* here. And then Trieste itself came into view. The hills of the city opened invitingly before me, the city where steamships once blew their horns for the girls on the shore, as the Triestine Slovene writer Boris Pahor describes in his novels. Just before the train rolled into the central station, I recalled the gently nostalgic *chiusa tristezza* sung by the Triestine Italian poet Umberto Saba in his poem "Tre vie" [Three streets]; I imagined the shuffling steps of Nora Joyce in one of the thirteen rented apartments through which her husband's creative madness raged—James Joyce taught English at the Berlitz School here. I listened in on the provocative debates among Triestine Slovene social democrats who, in the years before World War I, unsuccessfully argued for the establishment of the first-ever Slovene university in this cosmopolitan port rather than in provincial, land-locked Ljubljana. Though I could not actually see it, my mind envisioned the elegiac San Carlo Pier as it makes its appearance in several Slovene poems written in the 1920s and 1930s; I could not actually hear it, but mentally I eavesdropped on the hushed chatter of the Slovene women who every week used to come down the Istrian slopes to the marketplace in the harbor where they peddled their fresh produce—today you find them only in the contemporary fiction of the Slovene writer Marjan Tomšič. In the Santa Anna Cemetery, the epigraph on the grave of the Italian Triestine modernist Italo Svevo tells me that the novelist "smiles at the passing of life and glory which belatedly crowned his work," while the Austrian Triestine critic and publisher extraordinaire Roberto "Bobi" Bazlen whispers, from a desk in the Biblioteca Civica, that the only possible way to write a book is as a series of footnotes.

The geography of cities and ports, streets and plazas has always meant more to me than a mere tangle of little circles and lines on unfolded maps. Time and again it sends me on voyages through a literary terrain where I discover fragments of private meaning and footnotes to the daily onslaught of cultural signs. Indeed, I get the lay of the land through books and authors. But even I, a bastard of Guttenberg's galaxy, must consciously force myself not to see Trieste solely in the light of national stereotypes. This does not mean, of course, that there is no truth in the violent Fascist dimension of Trieste's past. The conversation I had with my wife about the city shows that, if one is to adopt an open mind toward history, one must first get rid of the pseudo-religious notion that there is only one proper way to understand the past. Many cultural critics today, at the beginning of the third millennium, like to mourn the demise of historical consciousness. Not only do they wring their hands over the loss of a single way of interpreting the past, but, above all, they lament the loss of a sense of history altogether as the present invades all other modes of time. The greater the amount of digitalized information, with ever more statistical tables and databases, the less capable we are, it seems, of engaging our own emotions, moral imagination, and critical reasoning, in order to actively shape our memory of things gone by.

There is, however, no past as such. There is no pure, Arcadian, prelapsarian past. All we are stuck with is the present tense glancing back over its shoulder. This is how we should approach the past: not wrapping it in our nostalgia but rather confronting it in a critical search for historical meaning. In other words, the kind of narrative liberties we inevitably take in reconstructing the past should help us better understand the transformative potential of our present situation and, possibly, articulate a vision of our future: "Tell me what you remember, and I will tell you what to expect." But we should bear in mind that the images of both the collective and the individual memory are never fixed, but change under the pressure of current need, as Andreas Huyssen so clearly explained in his inspiring *Twilight Memories.*

Ever since Freud and Nietzsche first shed light on the psychology and philosophy of history, we have been learning just how unreliable personal memory is, conditioned by pain and denial, suppression and evasion. Equally uncertain is the memory shared by an entire community. This kind of memory is kept not in personal diaries but rather in such things as public ceremonies. Most tangibly, the collective memory finds public expression through the rhetoric of stone, in a frozen cavalry of monuments and the towering grandeur of museums. Built of granite, marble, and concrete, monuments and museums promise continuity, but they are nonetheless erected on the quicksand of ideological platitudes. In many cases, the original intentions behind their creation have been lost, washed away in the river of time. Robert Musil, that brilliant chronicler of the declining Austro-Hungarian Empire, captured well the bitter aroma of such loss when he observed that there is nothing in the world as invisible as monuments.

No Place for Absolute Grace

The memorial plaques affixed to the various houses where Slovene cultural fig-ures of the past—writers, poets, publishers, grammarians—either were born or worked are invisible in just this way. These caryatids of collective memory have become a kind of "second nature" for us, pervading the map of Slovene cities, villages, and hamlets to such an extent that their original meanings have almost been forgotten.

One fleeting scene from recent memory, however, I have not forgotten. It happened in Old Ljubljana, the part of the city that dates back to the Middle Ages, in Jurčič Square, where the bourgeois swagger of New Square pauses for a moment in the open area that lies between the elegant Hribar Embankment and Jewish Lane, before the air is once more squeezed uneasily into a narrow gorge between rows of townhouses. Under the bust of Josip Jurčič, author of the first Slovene novel, a genre that did not emerge in my country until the mid-nineteenth century, a man barely in his twenties was explaining to his obviously foreign guest that the square was named after "a guy who got into literature be-cause he didn't know how to do politics." I was startled to hear this casual summary of local literary history. It was shaped, I suppose, by the unquestioned assumption that Slovene writers and poets of past were not really artists in the full sense of the word but rather something on the order of disguised and failed, if not phony, politicians. Such a belief goes hand in glove with the kind of blasé dismissal that reduces the literary life to little more than a convenient mask for political ambition.

This jaded shrug of the shoulders, it seems to me, perpetuates itself not only in the thinking of private individuals; it assails us, too, in Slovenia's mass media and from numerous public rostrums in our "society in transition." Whenever a writer tries to step into the post-communist "arena of life" and critically address social deformities, annoyed arbiters of popular taste shove him or her to the pe-riphery. After the independent nation-state of Slovenia was established in 1991, Slovenes supposedly no longer had any need for this sort of engaged art, now seen as hopelessly out of date and obsolete in the new society. Today, in inde-pendent Slovenia, the motto seems to be that writers should have nothing to do with the political and moral aspects of the collective life—for the simple reason that such involvement had been a routine part of the writer's job description before independence. Such a view makes writers out to be not only unwitting "beautiful losers" but, even more so, pathetic ones.

Anyone who questions such handy formulas is all too often accused of a self-serving nostalgia, pining for a time when the writer's words still meant something in the communal life. But it is not so easy to ignore lessons from the time when writers were valued as one of the few public voices bold enough to challenge the totalitarian order—a time when, to paraphrase Kafka, the lie be-came truth. I understand the grudge of those journalistic doctors of superficiality who, in the Slovene cultural arena of the 1990s, belittled the efforts of intellec-tuals and writers whose credo had been shaped in opposition to institutionalized "whitewashed sepulchres." These writers, after all, were not able to conform themselves overnight with the post-communist imperative of selective oblivion and start again from square one, as I described in my article "A Haven of Free Speech: The Story of *Nova revija* in Slovenia."

Warnings about the hydra of the ancien régime—which, some claim, survived the Velvet Revolutions of 1989 intact and is now once again sowing its dragon's seed of communist manipulation—are, of course, extremely unpleasant to those newly minted democrats who would rather not be reminded of their past exercise in ideological dressage. The cynicism of slow surrender, which regards any status quo as inevitable historical necessity, is the only logical consequence of renouncing the fragile, yet civilizing belief that the present is pregnant with the past and that those who forget history are doomed to repeat it. But drawing attention to catalogues of totalitarian distortions is troublesome from another perspective, too—one that offers little consolation to genuine critics of post-communism and even less to the legions of mayflies who, ever since the initial democratic elections of 1990, have been flinging themselves against an imaginary Colossus of communist continuity in the hope that their present critical buzzing will obscure their past civic servility.

The problem, I think, is that the anticommunist obsession precludes consideration of the rarely acknowledged fact that Slovenia had no classical dissidents, in the strict East European sense of the word. Nor was there any classical *samizdat*—a literary and cultural underground press—such as was typical for the former Warsaw Pact countries. The intricate dialectics of collaboration and resistance rendered the cultural sphere—in the unique "soft" communist conditions of Yugoslavia, which was not a member of Warsaw Pact—considerably more liberal than in the rest of Eastern Europe. Unfortunately, the characteristic rhythm of repressive tolerance, by means of which Yugoslav communist leaders obsessively looked for a "third way," not only socio-politically but also culturally, has not yet been properly researched. An honest examination of the collective mental anatomy might give some people enough courage to account for their own personal involvement, however limited, in the functioning of the former political order. Nevertheless, such a discussion appears only sporadically in Slovene intellectual journals. Critical reflection on the communist past might well reveal that the kind of absolutes posited by a utilitarian Manicheism of good and evil simply did not exist. There could be no certainties for those confused people who, even when they wanted to speak the truth, were never really sure whether their personal version had not somehow been already co-opted. The greatest strength of the totalitarian mind lies precisely in the cunning way it exacts absolute answers from anyone who challenges its dominance.

Exclusive extremist positions, founded as they are on self-interested claims about the past, can never acknowledge the basic fact that every document of culture is also a document of barbarism, as Walter Benjamin famously observed about the two-sidedness of historical narrative. It is not possible to "package" the past into a simplified lexicon of absolute good and absolute evil, where communism and anticommunism merely switch moral plus or minus signs, while the totalitarian substance of both remains identical.

Such absolutism sounds particularly improbable to anyone who came of age in the 1980s, as I did. By then, the communist regime was already loosening its grip and my generation felt rather fortunate, as I write in my essay *Twilight of the Idols: Recollections of a Lost Yugoslavia*. Nevertheless, those of us who wanted to get a comprehensive picture of the past had to scout out a number of materials that were not easily accessible because they were written by survivors of communist massacres and political refugees. These pamphlets, magazines, and books were, for the most part, printed by the Slovene ethnic communities in Austria and Italy or by Slovene anticommunist émigrés across the Atlantic. We almost never heard first-hand accounts of the past, except when Partisan veterans visited our grade school. But since these were officially organized encounters, no one took them very seriously. Still, it would be foolish to deny that the War for National Liberation and the communist-led resistance did serve as the main sources of narrative material for public rituals.

It is never an easy challenge to face the darker aspects of the collective memory. One needs the emotional and cognitive understanding that comes from the simultaneous reading of mutually exclusive explanations. This makes it possible to see, for example, that there were two separate Slovene armies during World War II: an anticommunist army on the one side and, on the other, the Partisan resistance movement controlled by Tito in the manner of a Stalinist Habsburg; that both the "Red" communist murderers, who were responsible for the indiscriminate postwar slaughter of local Nazi collaborators, and the "White" Fascist torturers fed on the same ruthless violence and messianic zeal; that, sadly, the Slovenian Home Guard's oath of fidelity to Hitler at the Ljubljana Stadium in 1943 was expressly different—not only because the Home Guard had received armaments from the Germans, but also on a symbolic level—from the situation in Poland, where anticommunist patriotic forces, staunchly supported by the Roman Catholic Church, managed to preserve their anti-Nazi stance and so kept the genie of civil war tightly shut away in its bottle. Just as the former communist executioners are incapable of admitting that murder cannot be justified by the noble idea of a classless earthly paradise—since such an admission would literally demolish the world in which they live—so, too, former Slovene "White" soldiers cannot raise questions about their collaboration with the Nazi occupation forces.

Many muffled rumors, spreading through informal channels, about "how things really were" challenged the official ideology of history. My doubts first stirred when I read the explosive interview with Edvard Kocbek (1904–1981), a former partisan leader and respected poet, which Boris Pahor published in 1975, in a little book that had to be printed in Trieste, outside the borders of socialist Slovenia. Kocbek, going against his former comrades, spoke of the most carefully guarded taboo in the official symbolic narrative—the large-scale postwar massacres—and accused the communists of committing unpardonable crimes. But it wasn't until the vehement public debates over national reconciliation in the 1980s that I gradually began to realize that there was much more to local history than the interpretation put forth by the victors. From special issues of intellectual magazines and from the irreverent political weeklies that were becoming more tolerated, I slowly pieced together another more disturbing and more ambiguous understanding of the Slovene experience of World War II. A liberation struggle against foreign occupation now was overlapping with a savage civil war, especially in the Italian-controlled *Provincia di Lubiana*. Beneath the threat of national annihilation, there was also fratricide: a horrible revelation.

It was perhaps then, in my college years, that I began to understand more precisely what was meant by the injunction that we must come to grips with the past as a whole so as to avoid repeating it. This involves confronting the blank spots in the collective history, its darker aspects and unsettling currents. What is more, a kind of moral maturity is at issue, which may be measured by the degree to which one actually *is* able to face conflicting communal narratives. To begin to talk about the totality of national existence is to begin to grasp the meaning of *hamartia*—the tragic error that, in its modern transformations, has more than once, and especially during World War II, divided the Slovene people and forced the public to consider what it means for someone to be "guilty without guilt." If a tragic situation can ever be resolved in catharsis, it must first be recognized as tragic.

The Myopic Politics of Aestheticism

Any single appropriation of the past that tries to replace all others is doomed to take on the rigidity of a monument whose original significance no longer speaks to the contemporary mind. Such thinking understands a truth to be *the* Truth, that is to say, to be the overarching idea in the name of which everything is permissible: erasures, censorship, silence, oblivion, death. To rebel against the dictatorship of oblivion means to grasp the totality of cultural memory. For me, at least, if no longer for the young man on Jurčič Square, some of the most important Slovene writers—from France Prešeren to Ivan Cankar, from Srečko Kosovel to Edvard Kocbek—remain accomplished artists even though they engaged in a confrontation with the collective national tradition. Their imaginative power catapults me into a separate universe, punches me in the stomach, and unleashes my dreams.

In the late 1990s, claims about the self-sufficiency of art became a predictable cliché in the intellectual debates taking place in Slovenia. After the collapse of the communist ancien régime, literature was not supposed to have any function other than what Kant characterized as disinterested pleasure and purposefulness without purpose. But recent efforts to liberate literature from the residual shackles of political, ideological, national, and social concerns are hardly the same as those made a quarter-century ago. At that time, the aesthetic dimension of art could not be openly discussed precisely because of such concerns; the defense of the aesthetic dimension of art was, therefore, perfectly justified. But today, it seems that the aesthetic function alone is supposed to constitute the work of art. I may be a disappointed romantic, but I don't agree. My faith in the totality of the artistic vision finds confirmation in John Keats's well-known letter of February 3, 1818 to J. H. Reynolds:

> Poetry should be great and unobtrusive, a thing which enters into one's soul, and does not startle it or amaze it with itself, but with its subject—how beautiful are the retired flowers! how would they lose their beauty were they to throng into the highway crying out, "admire me I am a violet!—dote upon me I am a primrose!"

Aestheticism prefers to exhaust itself in technical questions about the artwork's composition, narrative structure, idiomatic strategies, and so on. The truth it propounds sooner or later boils down to the truth of the shining form, marketing the empty shell as if it were in itself a supreme creative achievement. It is, of course, deceptively simple to defend such a position with a cool shrug of the shoulders: "You don't understand hermetic verse? Too bad for you!" Of course, there can be no discussion about the divine spark that inspires the poet. But I cannot reconcile myself to the kind of diluted modernism that today passes for artistic excellence, taking the once liberating, but now crippling doctrine of "a norm without a norm" to the point where no one dare say the emperor has no clothes—say, that is, that aestheticist art offers precious little that might compel, engage, or move us. Perhaps Czesław Miłosz provides the most pointed condemnation of formalistic game-playing when he states: "Form has several uses in poetry, one of them being that, like freezing, it can preserve 'spoiled meat'" (cited in Robert Hass's *Twentieth Century Pleasures*).

Aestheticism makes much hay of its illustrious predecessors, who radicalized writing, broke the iron hold of tradition, and transgressed known boundaries. But such reference to the formal experiments in the works of Paul Célan, T. S. Eliot, and Gustave Flaubert conveniently forgets that each of these writers testified in his own way to the existential, social, and moral conflicts of the age. Is it really possible to ignore the parallel between the shards of traditional verse form and the ruins of European humanism, as the Holocaust looms large in Célan's mournful *Totenfuge*? Can one ignore the fact that the visionary audacity of *The Waste Land* was necessary—not so the poem could bask in the sunlight of its own innovation, but rather to breathe life into the cacophony of history in a work that can stand for the whole twentieth century? And does not *Madame Bovary*, with its wonderfully mundane dialectic of virtue and guilt, emotional tremor and bourgeois hypocrisy, manage to distill the universal truth of an age, in which we recognize not only the empire of Napoleon III but our own time as well?

Formalist aestheticism is, like every kind of absolutism, merely an offshoot of the parochial mind. In antiquity, they knew that one must be wary of the "man of one book." All things are clear to him, since for him there exists but a single truth. Like prophets of "the one and only" truth, advocates of latter-day aestheticism can never penetrate the cosmopolitan artistic imagination, where a challenging mix of styles, languages, biographies, and experiences creates the conditions for the emergence of genuine artworks which live beyond their own age precisely because they bear witness to it in a way that is universal. Theoretical interpretation that responds to social, national, or political allusions in an artwork by neurotically exclaiming "Get thee behind me, Satan!" only contributes to a politics of artistic ghettoization. Formalist aestheticism tries to obfuscate the fact that in an artwork, the artist brings together a variety of existential, social, and national aspects of experience in a search for meaningful balance. The blindness of formalist aestheticist critics, then, serves the same goal as the pretensions of the post-communist political elite, who aim to relegate writers, once the most outspoken witnesses of their time, to a velvet prison of pure textuality. From the narrow windows of their ivory tower, writers would no longer be able to observe matters relating to the common public life. This is the ultimate goal, too, of any effort to ghettoize artistic language.

Art as Vision and Testimony

The affinity between art and life should not be hard to grasp. So much early-twentieth-century Central European writing reveals it: the poignant verses of Georg Trakl, the deadpan humor of Jaroslav Hašek, the learned essays of Herman Broch—all provide avenues into the historical convulsions that, after the labor pains of World War I and the collapse of the Austro-Hungarian Empire, gave birth to a new map of Europe, a post-imperial Europe with numerous new nation-states. Something more than mere images of individual bewilderment can be found in what these poets of disintegration offer us, readers who witnessed at the end of twentieth century a repetition of the traumatic catastrophes that shook its beginning. These writers offer us dark premonitions of a barbaric Europe—*Barbaropa*, as Albert Ehrenstein, the tragic voice of Austrian expressionism, termed the machinery of military and political power. (Ehrenstein, by the way, once respected for his radical leftist stance, became for that very reason persona non grata in post–World War II Vienna; he died forgotten in a New York hospice in 1950.)

Memorable writers are both the eyewitnesses of their time and visionaries who transcend it. The whisper of poetry cannot hold back the very real flow of history, but it can illuminate it in such a way that the reader understands that, in any good poem or novel, *de te fabula narratur* "the story tells about you." That the story, in a compelling work of literature does, indeed, "tell about you" can be seen in the recent books of two leading Slovene poets, both of whom have created bodies of work long considered paragons of pure textuality. Tomaž Šalamun and Boris A. Novak earned their reputations by exploring formal structure. Šalamun put so much avant-garde imagination, radical linguistic "estrangement," and lyric originality into the traditional verse cage that many of the poets who followed his intoxicating trail have not yet recovered from the curse of epigonic apprenticeship. Novak's poetic approach, meanwhile, is marked by the very opposite. He has attempted to restore much of the traditional formal discipline, technical craftsmanship, and metrical skill which Šalamun's imitators, in the name of their own impotence, simply proclaimed to be unnecessary burdens. In short, for both poets, external reality is less of a concern, since their aesthetic impulses lie in the renewal of an autonomous idiom. Nevertheless, their recent books demonstrate that the sign of a great poet is primarily the ability to respond to the existential challenge of the age by seeking to create an appropriate aesthetic iconography for it.

> The borders of the countries on the earth's crust
> hold less than the frostwork on my window. The tree
> gets dressed. Breaks. You whisper and splash with ice.
> I hug you and brush you.
>   *(Translated by the poet and Christopher Merrill)*

Thus writes Šalamun in the poem "Versailles," included in his 1995 collection *Ambergris* [Ambra] and published in English translation in *The Four Questions of Melancholy*. A poet whose work and biography have from the start been tautly joined in a single whole, Šalamun shows us that the truth of the world is hardly a matter of form in itself. The poem conveys—gently but assuredly—a picture of the brutal whirlpool that sucks us in day and night. It hints at the skeleton of today's Barbaropa for all of us, both for those who try to look into the face of the Medusa and those who avert their eyes from the violent chaos. We may flee from the lyric image, but we cannot hide. The living nightmare of Barbaropa, dreamed by towns and villages throughout the mountains of the Balkans and the forests of the Caucasus, seeps slowly from isolated "scenes of conflict" into the brains of individuals. Medieval maps, to indicate places unknown where cartographers had not yet managed—or dared—to explore, used a phrase that suggested a threatening force: *ubi leones*, "where lions are." There are no unknown places left on the contemporary globe, but that does not mean that the lions' lands have disappeared.

On the contrary, the lions are everywhere, as both Šalamun and Novak reveal in their poetry. The world is dominated by a politics of *cold peace,* whose rule cannot be controlled even by its architects and where concerns about human rights violations are liable to be transformed into a Pilate-like washing of hands. Shouting about the unacceptability of violence often unwittingly helps blur the moral distinction between the attackers' ruthlessness and the defenders' desperate resistance, promoting impotence as a desirable political stance. The ritualized neutrality to which the greater part of Western governments succumbed during the wars of Yugoslav succession in the 1990s is, in my dispirited view, an embodiment of such impotence. As a result, the cancer of national self-aggrandizement not only was allowed to consume the Balkans, its presence in the very heart of Europe could not be concealed, either.

In "Versailles," Šalamun shows no interest in the "progressive" conspiracy theory, which customarily asserts that the "new world disorder" is nothing other than the domination of transnational capital. Nor is he interested in its counterpart, the "conservative" theory that war is the natural state of affairs and that the world is a cauldron of evil where balance is maintained by a continual transfer of lethal conflicts from one place to another. The poet's voice is, instead, founded on the inner assurance of a seer, not on the external strategies of a political analyst. Here lies the poet's infinite advantage. For only an artist can know, intuitively, that "all tears will be weighed on Judgment Day" as Émile Cioran wrote during his Paris exile. The associative universe of meaning revealed in "Versailles" tugs us inevitably toward the realization that the poem's message about changed borders is intended for us, is truly "our story." Unreliable political and national maps are all we are left with. At the same time, the poem alludes to the stench of death rising from a vague yet persistent feeling that the bombed-out Presidential Palace in Chechnya and the charred houses of Sarajevo are, in a sense, memento mori aimed at a political neutrality run amok.

Boris A. Novak's book *The Master of Insomnia* [Mojster nespečnosti] (1995) contains an obligation of similar moral timbre. The polished verses that interweave the poet's command of form with the personal witness of a tormented man, hold a key to the riddle of modern history. Even when Novak writes the testament of a happy childhood, the artist's only homeland, he revives the prophecy of Cassandra. For Novak, the poet does indeed dwell in an ivory tower, but not in order to escape the historical drama, as the advocates of a stunted aestheticism would have it. Rather, he climbs up there, in the poem "The Ivory Tower" [Slonokoščeni stolp], to bear witness:

> From here one sees far: with the gift of a bird
> I will be the first to know when the mob approaches.
> Things have a calm and terrible face.
>
> *(Translated by Rawley Grau)*

The poet's personal story is more vivid than any sort of history written in geopolitical think-tanks, for his is the only voice that does not hesitate to speak the truth: that the story of an individual is always the story of the world, too. Novak's play with verse structure, from the Italian *sonetto caudato* (the "tailed" sonnet, with fourteen lines plus a coda) to the French triolet, is no mere exercise of skill, but rather an aesthetically provocative attempt to demonstrate that only the formal perfection of a poem can reveal the horrifying imperfection of the world.

His testimonies concerning Sarajevo, the Dalmatian sea coast, a child's room, his father (a Partisan veteran), the indifferent passing of time, and the desperate pain of loss—all confirm Walter Benjamin's sad observation that the substance is hidden in details we usually overlook when we try to see "the big picture." The poet is not really interested in the big picture. And that is as it should be. He has been awake too long, attentively gathering forgotten slices of past time and present cruelty, which he tries to rescue from oblivion. He is "the master of insomnia" because the destruction does not let him sleep. Not for a moment does he let himself be drawn into the magic circle of frivolous ornamentation. Eyes wide open, he observes both the beauty of creation and the horror of destruction, of doing and undoing. The categorical imperative to look, to

sing, to be, gives Novak a bitter maturity that has bid farewell to all social delusions and the maneuvers of reason. He offers only the sobering knowledge that
murder has again become the foundation of the world and that flowers bloom
not from a need to create beauty but as a means of survival. Surely I am not the
only one who catches a glimpse of my own despair and paralysis, and my own
defeat, in the final lines of Novak's elegy "Doing and Undoing" [Dejanje in
razdejanje]:

> Everyone penetrates foreign spaces.
> Grass overgrows graves and grasslands.
> One must be strong. I cannot.
>
> *(Translated by Rawley Grau)*

The theory of pure textuality, whereby an artwork becomes valuable only
when it has freed itself of any association with external reality, takes us in a
completely opposite direction, totally different from one that seeks connections
between art and life, as do these poems of Šalamun and Novak. Yet, despite the
dramatic changes in post-communist society, the lackeys of the aestheticist
canon calmly continue with "business as usual." A grind mill of specialized
quarterlies, book reviews, and literary supplements in mass-market newspapers
still churns out the same old pulp time and again as if the world in which we
live—both as individuals and as a national collective—is not fundamentally
different from the one in which that theory was conceived with such critical élan
and, in the case of Slovenia, political boldness. In a catatonic agony of grandeur,
the gurus of contemporary aestheticism keep on repeating their mantra: "Art is
autonomous and has no connection with the problems of politics (society, nation, the planet, technology, etc.)."

But haven't we heard all this a hundred times already? Surely today even
high-school students understand that autonomy is a necessary but not sufficient
condition for the creation of a genuine work of art. This simple assertion should
be, in my opinion, the starting point for a consideration of the existential meaning of style in a literary work, not its sad culmination. If we stop here, we can
only fall back powerless before a blurred infinity of allusions and ambiguities,
which the artwork thrives on even as it moves away from the immediate reality
in which it originated. In their pathological flight from the bridge that joins the
individual artwork to the life of the larger community, aestheticist critics are no
better than neoliberal political theorists.

Politically, I am a freethinker—*Freigeist*—if such a hopelessly naïve attitude is at all possible today. I find support for this attitude in the Enlightenment
traditions of civil and human rights, the democratic social order, the priority of
the individual, and respect for differences. I am all the more distressed, then, by
neoliberal rhetoric, which continually spins its prayer wheel of stereotypes,
leaving no room, for example, for any skeptical thought about the scope and
purpose of national identity. Yes, national identity, that troublesome accident of
birth, that bathos-soaked enthusiasm, that outdated nineteenth-century mindset!
I know them by heart, these predictable objections from the neoliberal cate-

chism, for which any form of national sentiment is merely a cover for chauvinism, that is, for the insanity that views one's own nation as a chosen and superior people—as *the* Nation. I, too, am often uncomfortable with such nationalist pontification.

But I cannot understand why neoliberals should have to concede key dimensions of human existence—in advance and without any critical engagement—to those conservative claims in which the personal search for meaning is codified into theological dogma, delight in family gives way to a commandment about one's duty to procreate, and nationality petrifies into an absolute. It fills me with melancholy to see how neoliberal thought leaves the answers to the central question of modern life—the question of belonging—to the watchful gatekeepers of tradition. It is the neoliberal position that loses most when its advocates fail to understand that the definition of the human condition—which is more than an unconnected series of random events between birth and death— is not automatically the domain of parish sermons. It is the neoliberals who are on the losing side when they are unable to grasp that, just because you acknowledge the right to create alternative forms of family, it does not mean you must repudiate the nuclear family as an unconditionally patriarchal institution—when they do not realize how terribly mistaken is any approach that sees national identity as a mask for latent fascism.

The Social Meaning of the Slovene Neo-Avant-Garde

Aestheticism can do little more than demonstrate its own blindness to the fact that a genuine work of art must always bear subjective witness to its own era and, at the same time, reveal the universal human condition. The aestheticist critic quickly forgets, for instance, that what makes Shakespeare's plays attractive in any historical period is their universal grasp of ideals and values, mediated and reconfigured through the body of the individual. The great Elizabethan playwright wrote about the moral, social, and political controversies of his day quite unambiguously, so that his contemporaries were able to find in his plays direct commentary on external reality. But we, too, who are more or less unfamiliar with Shakespeare's original context, still read his work with undivided attention and the kind of thrill one gets when confronting a mystery. It is the metaphysical "surplus" that makes his texts soar far above the ephemeral op-ed columns in yesterday's newspaper.

To give a concrete example, in contemporary Slovene cultural life there persists a particular aestheticist dogma. Having completely rejected the engaged politics and poetics of a critical "dissident" generation, proponents of aestheticism have gone to the other extreme. They are mainly gathered around the monthly journal *Literatura*, although their ideas have found a way to other prominent media institutions, as well. The basic feature of this dogma springs from a reductive reading of the recent cultural past. Seeking support for a defense of the free imagination, critics and writers in the aestheticist vein often turn to the work of Dušan Pirjevec (1921–1977), a charismatic Heideggerian professor of literature who authored an influential defense of art in the seventies. His essay, *The Question of Poetry, the Question of Nation* [Vprašanje o poeziji, vprašanje naroda] (1978), hotly debated in both elite political forums and oppositional writers' circles alike, developed the complex concept of the "artistic blockade." This term refers to the historical imperative of Romantic national consciousness-raising in traditional Slovene literature, which, as a result, failed to fully realize its autonomous imaginative potential. Literature was thus torn between service to the Muses and service to the Nation.

In the 1970s, this was a profoundly liberating insight. In that period, the guardians of sentimental humanism demanded only one thing of neo-avant-garde artists: that they harness their works to the nationalist cause. Pirjevec, in his argument that art must first be responsible to its own inner nature, explicitly defended the right of the creative impulse to speak however it wanted. Starting with the principle of freedom—which in the political context of Slovenia at the time was far from being a given—Pirjevec outlined a coherent theoretical basis for the artistic imagination that transcended all prescriptions, whether of a political, national, or ideological nature. Pirjevec attempted to make the appointed arbiters of public taste understand the necessity of autonomy for art—a principle that Western art had discovered at the end of the seventeenth century, when it divested itself of the patronage of the church and the aristocracy (as I discussed in my essay *Reluctant Modernity*).

Despite the efforts of leading writers, the Yugoslav communist regime for a long time refused to hear anything about artistic autonomy. The first books of postwar modernist poetry had to be self-published because they refused to conform to the red horizons of dictated optimism and thus could not receive the state's imprimatur. The Yugoslav Communist Party, however, gradually relinquished its direct interference and, in late 1950s, moved away from total control over the arts. Two decades later, Pirjevec's work signaled a triumph for autonomous art. The relaxed cultural atmosphere among critical intellectuals in the 1960s and 1970s bolstered his theoretical stand.

The philosophical structuralism and psychoanalysis that later propelled Slavoj Žižek to international intellectual stardom, the widely read translation of Hugo Friedrich's *The Structure of the Modern Lyric*—the bible of immanent criticism—which aimed the heavy guns of German academic scholarship at then-justified targets of positivism, Roland Barthes's famous essay on "the death of the author," published in the radical quarterly *Problemi*—all these intellectual currents helped create conditions that allowed art as art to take up residence (somewhat belatedly) in Slovenia. But the Pirjevec school was the driving force that steered the cultural elite away from social and national considerations and toward the freedom of the artistic imagination.

Looking back at the 1970s, however, it seems wise to ask whether the free artistic imagination really was so "separate" from what was transpiring in the society at large? Of course, if one relied on the methodological crutches of aestheticism, one would have to believe that such a separation was a fait accompli.

After all, aestheticism rejects on principle the idea that, for instance, some aspect of the author's biography might possibly reveal a way into the origins and character of his art. Mild contempt is also accorded social history and the history of ideas, which attempt to locate the individual artwork within larger cultural and political processes. Aestheticism begins, indeed, with the conviction that art hovers in a vacuum of celestial spheres with no connection whatsoever to the circumstances surrounding its own birth. For such critics, any artistic depiction of "the panorama of sterility and anarchy that is history" (T. S. Eliot) must remain alien.

I beg to differ. In my opinion, the neo-avant-garde endeavors in Slovenia were not entirely devoid of political character. Their political implications can best be understood when we consider the social context in which these works—through their abstract textual architecture, dense surrealist imagery, and modes of irony—waged battle on two fronts: engagement and indifference. They either renounced the straitjacket of sentimental humanism, with its concomitant ideological directives about faith in a better future, or they completely ignored it. Engaged artistic idioms sought to critically examine the manipulative strategies of power. The poetics of indifference, on the other hand, embodied a conviction that the artist's withdrawal into the private sphere was in itself political insofar as it tried to preserve an open space of free choice in a land where external freedom was impossible. For it was not, in fact, possible to attain freedom under the conditions that reigned in Yugoslavia during the totalitarian "leaden seventies"—a period that saw the inglorious end of the short-lived student occupation of the School of the Arts building at the University of Ljubljana, a purge among dissenting university professors, and the reinforcement of media censorship.

But today, throughout post-communist Europe, the situation is completely different, and Slovenia is no exception. Here, too, countless forms of freedom force themselves upon us from the emptiness of television screens and gigantic billboards. Postmodernism is the common denominator. As an artistic style, it captured the *Zeitgeist* with its chain of self-reflective references that deliberately left out messy emotion, conflicted moral reflection, and existential tremor. Postmodernism in Slovene literature found its most enthusiastic adherents, myself included, among the young writers of *Literatura*. The convention of blurred genres become the dominant mode in the 1980s. As an artistic style, postmodernism lasted barely a decade. But as a general cultural attitude, postmodernism has become an entrenched mode of communication and understanding and continues to percolate in the mass media. Its aestheticist self-involvement signifies a vacant, if perhaps refined, spirit—so presciently predicted by Karl Mannheim in *Ideology and Utopia* (1929): "It is possible that in the future, in a world where nothing is ever new anymore and where everything has been done, a situation will exist in which thought is utterly devoid of all ideological and utopian elements."

Mannheim's prophecy seems particularly fitting for those charlatans of today's "anything goes" philosophy who try to convince us that we live in a redeemed world where nothing is binding anymore since everything is permitted.

With a newly won political freedom, ecumenical indifference to various artistic styles, and even the presumed end of the national question, we urgently need to ask ourselves once more: Just what does aestheticism really signify? What sort of meaning can there be in a self-sufficient glass bead game? And what, after all, is the existential charge of an artwork that does not want to have anything to do with either the author's or the reader's experience? Such works respond to the age with voluntary silence, refusing to vibrate on the wavelength of shifting historical, national, and social movements. These movements are far from the happy triumph of "post-history" that Francis Fukuyama—in accordance with the omnipresent illusion that liberal democracy had become the sole world system—proposed at the promising start of the Velvet Revolutions in Eastern Europe.

From this angle, today's mesmerized repetition of Pirjevec's claim about the requisite autonomy of art, today hardened into orthodoxy, seems a pale substitute for a responsible, if perhaps dangerous, search for new answers to new challenges.

The Conflicted Legacy of Modernism

If nothing else, its own recent history obliges art and literature to correspond with the spirit of the age. Post–World War II art did not, after all, arise in a social or moral vacuum. Existentialism was born in response to the senselessness of genocide and war. In Slovenia, it achieved its greatest expression in the arrested horror found in the poems of Dane Zajc and Gregor Strniša. The writers of the French *nouveau roman* and their Slovene disciples strove for dispassionate description, beyond the dramaturgical rules of storyline and character psychology. They used these strategies not because they were abandoning all commentary on actual social-historical forces, but rather because they wanted to renounce the humanistic ideal of depth. They viewed traditional metaphysics and the political economy of the bourgeoisie as largely responsible for the world's metamorphosis into a wasteland. That is, they saw humanism as a manifestation of nihilism.

Every trend in the postwar history of West European and, a small step behind, Slovene literature derives from the heritage of elite modernism. In its rejection of nineteenth-century norms, modernist art presupposed, as Stephane Mallarmé said, the personal risk (economy) and critical challenge (poetry) necessary for the construction of alternative worlds. But postmodernism is uncomfortable with either personal risk or critical challenge. In the happy Babylon of postmodern pluralism, equal value is generously bestowed on all forms of expression. A billboard ad for a cute little Renault Clio, the novels of Gabriel García Márquez, an anarchist bumper sticker, the hallucinations of religious fundamentalists, the symbol of a pissing boy on the restroom door, a papal homily, the witty speech balloons of Magnus and Bunker's *Alan Ford* comic strip— these are all just "texts" with, allegedly, no substantive moral, political, or artistic difference between them. What is more, should anyone dare to suggest that, yes, all these phenomena, statements, and viewpoints might indeed be equal in principle (they all have an equal right to be expressed), but that does not mean their contents are of equal value—that person risks, at the very least, casual disdain, if not outright banishment from intellectual circles. Today, after all, everyone knows that there is no longer any ultimate authority, God is dead, no one has a mandate over truth, blah, blah, blah. . .

Such a fundamental change in the way we receive messages has, of course, serious consequences for the social status of contemporary art. The orgy of demands for equal rights in theory and, at the same time, equal value for all forms of aesthetic expression in practice has, I believe, weakened the creative integrity and symbolic validity of works of art. The other, that which is outside of art, is condemned to disappear if everything around us is treated as aesthetic expression. Contemporary art that does not want to drown in the aesthetization of everyday life has two options, both bad. The first is for art to turn to forgotten neoclassicist and pseudo-mythic imagery. Under this option, art employs images that are alien to a large majority of the public. The postmodern absence of tension between history and myth, which was the cognitive basis of modernism, thus becomes, sadly, entirely logical. All the hodgepodge pseudo-mythic imagery of postmodern art acts as a non-obligatory sign of high culture, that is, as a social symbol with little substantive value.

American pop art, which many theorists see as the first postmodern art movement, provides a good example of the second option. With its appropriation of cheap reproduction techniques, such as silk-screening, and mass-culture products transformed into art commodities (Superman, Brillo pads, Campbell's Soup cans), pop art was hardly concerned with the critical analysis or representation of social conflict; all it did was hold an indifferent mirror up to them. Pop art did not intend to shock, transcend, provoke, or challenge; it was content simply to reproduce a reality that had already been reproduced by the media many times over. What is more, the leading American pop artists (e.g., Andy Warhol and Roy Lichtenstein) came to art by way of corporate marketing and mass advertising, bringing with them something totally new for art at the time: the brazen pretensions of commercial entrepreneurship. So there was nothing unusual about the fact that their guiding concern was how to get the best price for their services, as Raphael Sassower and Louis Cicotello remark in their book *The Golden Avant-Garde.*

Pop art's indifference to the negative-critical potential of modernism and its celebration of commercial success show that it is, indeed, a form of postmodern art. It appropriated only the formal technique of the historical avant-garde, while it disregarded its emancipatory program. The debt that contemporary art continues to pay to avant-garde excesses can be understood, then, primarily as a way for it to define itself—both, in the affirmative and the negative—against the creative achievements of surrealism, dadaism, constructivism, and futurism.

The Aesthetization of the Everyday World

A palette of enervated hopes that "everyone will write poetry," a zeal for taking beauty out of dusty museums and bringing it to the masses, a burning conviction that a revolution in aesthetics will lead to a social revolution in which bourgeois taste is replaced by an open appreciation for a form of art that melds with the everyday life of a free society—all these aspirations one finds in the manifestos of the historical avant-garde. And that is just where they remain today. But because this is where they were first articulated, they shine even today like a lighthouse firmly planted on the shores of modern art. Some contemporary artists are still enticed by such hopes; others have turned their back on them and in wobbly single-seaters explore the labyrinths of their own mind. Contemporary art either greets the endeavors of the historical avant-garde with silence or eagerly imitates them, but in a new context. One way or the other, it must respond to the challenge of the historical avant-garde.

Consider, for instance, the Slovene "retro-garde." The art collective Neue Slowenische Kunst (NSK) has been a major feature on the Slovene cultural landscape ever since its inception in the early 1980s. It represents a formidable enterprise with divisions devoted to practical philosophy, music, theater, design, and visual arts, all of which together conspired to create a virtual nation-state, complete with passports, embassies, and flags. The controversial activities of this group, however, cannot be properly understood without, at least, a cursory familiarity with the imaginative modes of provocation that characterized the avant-garde in the early twentieth century, both in Europe generally and on Slovene territory in particular. The emergence of avant-garde performances, in collision with the parochial social, political, and national conditions of Slovenia in the 1920s, has been helpfully analyzed by Lev Kreft in his contribution to the book *Central European Avant-Gardes: Exchange and Transformation, 1910–1930*. NSK proclaimed itself heir to this radical tradition and industriously adapted avant-garde techniques for its own ends, along with offering a critical paraphrase of a more recent Slovene predecessor, the 1960s art group OHO. Smartly conceived, precisely executed, and efficiently administered, this fascinating art collective, with its entourage of patrons, cheerleaders, hangers-on, admirers, and interpreters, was an important step forward for the Slovene cultural scene in the 1980s. Indeed, NSK was Slovenia's first internationally successful entry into postmodernism, as Inke Arns has discussed in a recent comprehensive analysis of the group.

But things have changed since the rise of NSK. Postmodernism is no longer a *terra incognita*, even less, a fashionable whim or intriguing novelty. In the late 1980s, when I wrote *Postmodern Sphinx*, my critical contribution to the domestication of postmodern ideas in Slovenia, things had not quite reached this point. At that time, the courageous artists of NSK were still having some unpleasant, if no longer frequent, run-ins with the communist authorities. Today, however, the democratic Slovene nation-state wears NSK like a flower in its lapel. Such total, if belated, recognition on the part of cultural officials shows just how decisively postmodernism has become part and parcel of the country's "house inventory." But this shows all the more clearly that postmodernism achieved only half the program set forth by the historical avant-garde: art *was* taken to the streets.

One of the important socio-historical processes that made postmodernism possible was the global aesthetization of everyday life. This process is characterized, above all, by a blurring of the distinction between the pragmatic and artistic dimensions. We see it in the phenomenon of the megastore, to take an obvious example. With many departments and an immense variety of merchandise, the megastore surpasses even the polymorphous delights of the postmodern novel. As Russell Berman compellingly observes in his *Modern Culture and Critical Theory,* the pre-aesthetic dimension of social life today scarcely exists, as the social order itself has become dependent on aesthetic design: the authentic human experience of a splashing waterfall is rendered unsatisfying in comparison with the over-designed nature photographs in Sierra Club calendars. With the total aesthetization of life, independent critical art, so characteristic of modernism, lost its special status as a realm in which the individual could imaginatively experience or mentally grasp utopian ideals about the promise of happiness. The private individual's intellectual and emotional efforts to understand the enigma of the artwork, are clearly no longer important in postmodernism. They have been replaced by the public appraisal of the artwork's market value. Postmodern art is no longer the embodiment of an alternative world that derives meaning from its aesthetic and ethical tensions with the existing order; on the contrary, postmodern art by and large supports, maintains, and justifies the existing order.

Given the disappearance of the distinction between art and the exterior world, we could say that modern developed societies are no longer based on the fabled work ethic, but instead are driven by the constantly churning engine of *commodity aesthetics.* Indeed, all products for mass consumption—watched over by a priestly council of industrial designers, professional propagandists, and public relations and market communications experts—are created in accordance with an aesthetic code. That is to say, they comply with the organic illusion of harmony and attractive shape, the signature component of *capitalist realism.* This is perhaps even more pernicious than socialist realism, its outdated counterpart, which up through the 1960s was the enforced aesthetic orthodoxy of the totalitarian regimes in Eastern Europe. Capitalist realism is more pernicious, for it insinuates itself into the minds of consumers as it beguiles them, with increasing success, into replacing any meditation on the beautiful and the good with the enjoyment of beautiful consumer goods. In the process it commodifies not only the products themselves but the mental frame within which the enjoyment of them takes place. The most this illusion can do is provide a formal fascination, which can no longer be compelling on an existential level.

Paradoxically, the aesthetization of the modern world finds additional support in any theory of textuality that does not critically account for the dynamics of actual social life. Such an approach is hardly an innocuous game. The decision to understand virtually everything as an aesthetic phenomenon, and so to abstain from grappling with questions of the good and the true, is an artistic decision. Conceived within the white cubes of the art world, it has, alas, become characteristic for entire societies, as the Bosnian writer Dževad Karahasan charged in *Sarajevo, Exodus of a City,* as he rejected the leveling of the diversity of human experience to mere aesthetic spectacle. If the whole universe gets reduced to special-effects fireworks, gratifying only our immediate need for sensual excitement, aestheticism risks becoming little more than a banal justification of the status quo.

Of course, I am not saying that people who advocate aestheticism are themselves to be blamed for the current calamities in international affairs. Pretentiousness is one thing, stupidity another. I am only saying that whenever critics scoff at the pursuit of personal commentary, utopian critique, or moral deliberation in a work of art, they ultimately collaborate in the promotion of the idea that art is but frivolous chatter. Critical focus solely on the aesthetic layer of the work of art will necessarily ignore the many different dialects of creative discourse that strive to bear witness to a more profound dimension of the world.

A Plea for an Expansive Story

In this regard, post-independence Slovene literature is engulfed in a new obscurity. My impression is that many Slovene writers have renounced any ambition to create expansive epic frescoes about the "here and now." Such an admittedly old-fashioned ambition goes hand in hand with a comprehensive aesthetic vision that strives to capture in a single text societal commotion and tectonic political changes. Lyric poetry is not enough, even if it is, arguably, more aesthetically accomplished than prose, as Robert Murray Davis, among others, intimated in his essay "Slovene Writing After Independence" (2001). A novel is required for the task I have in mind—the kind of novel that will have to forget metafictional trompe l'oeil. It will not be so interested in the dark chambers inside one's head—which is where the Slovene masters of the short story have locked themselves away (perhaps following the lead of Raymond Carver and literary minimalism). This kind of novel will report, instead, on what is happening on the streets and highways, at diplomatic banquets and in the board rooms of the frenzied post-communist business world. In this kind of novel, the "arena of life" will not be limited to the bedroom; instead, its characters will step outside into the world, a dangerous, morbid, dirty world of everyday manipulation—a world full of failed attempts to attain meaning, community, and human commitment.

I am not saying that contemporary Slovene writers are not good at what they do. On the contrary, it is exciting to see that narrative skills are at a much higher level among today's writers than they were at the beginning of twentieth century. Still, as an enthusiastic reader a little out of breath from all the new trends, I miss the kind of dramatic story structure I find in the novels of Faulkner, Hemingway, and Dos Passos, to name some shopworn examples. Even those all-too-rare Slovene literary works that try to depict the convulsions of the post-communist transition and independence tend to slip into the fixed mentality of Slovene dualism, that is, a dichotomy between aestheticist (good) and socially engaged (bad) writing. Under the pressure of this dualistic mentality, the work necessarily flattens into simplifications. But to create full-blooded literature it is not enough "to have balls," as Danilo Kiš observed in *Homo Poeticus*. In his own short stories, this excellent Serbian writer combined the glint of the post-modern mirrors he borrowed from Borges with a convincing description of the social and historical anomalies of totalitarianism.

The present image of Slovenian society in transition has not yet managed to crystallize in the novel the way the Great Depression of the 1930s did in American writing. A recognition of the crisis at hand, and of art's obligation to speak about its social consequences, brought together American writers of all stripes—leftists and conservatives, East Coast cosmopolitans and rural Southern writers. They posed such important questions as: What has caused the disintegration of moral values? What is poverty like and who is responsible for it? What are its repercussions for the individual soul? What opportunities are available at a time of social turbulence? The laboratory of post-communism is an ideal topic for any ambitious writer able to give aesthetic shape to the existential *frisson* of the individual against a background of social changes, the meaning of which remains unclear.

The Primordial Archetype of the City

It was Ivan Cankar who, at the dawn of the twentieth century, presciently described the meaning of the collective existence. What?!—I hear my compatriots exclaim—Cankar?! Cankar is obsolete! A big yawn! Hopelessly passé!

Ivan Cankar (1876–1918), the father of Slovene literary modernism, whose face adorns largest-denomination banknote of independent Slovenia and whose name is enshrined in the central cultural institution of the nation (Cankarjev Dom, "The Cankar Center"), is hardly in fashion today. His writings languish in schoolbooks, safely canonized, no longer present in contemporary Slovene consciousness. For the most part, they are viewed only as the discreet object of desire for provincial schoolteachers. But it would be shortsighted to dismiss the work of this first-rate Slovene writer with some cliché about the "blocked subjectivity" that supposedly kept him from reaching the aesthetic heights because he was thought to be overly concerned with the habits of the collective life.

Cankar was indeed troubled by the ligature between subjective and collective experience. He was keenly aware that his fate as an artist was intertwined with the fate of the national community, its social tumults and moral doubts, as well as with the chains with which the group mentality shackled an individual's heretical vision. When, at the end of 1909, Cankar returned from Vienna into the oppressively loving arms of Ljubljana—a return to "the center of life," he said—he cut the umbilical cord with the imperial capital, where he had spent his most artistically prolific decade. "I am worse than dust blowing in the wind," the young Cankar had written, much earlier, to his first lover, high on the conviction that "I come alive when I come home." This trembling cadence of yearning betrays the youthful soul and attachment to his homeland—despite a volcanic passion for disdaining it. "Oh, how I long for home (just think!) like an old man longs for his youth," he lamented—and dealt with his homesickness by writing a critique of Slovene petit bourgeois mores.

Although for a number of years he kept putting off his final return to Ljubljana, Cankar was guided by the light of the archetypal symbol of home, to which he devoted himself while living in Ottakring, one of Vienna's working-class neighborhoods. Cankar was keenly aware that the tensions between personal identity and the larger community are best expressed in literary pictures of the city as a metaphor for the world stage, as the "center of life." In this endeavor, Cankar was animated by a rich European literature, in which the urban culture of the *polis* managed to outweigh the advantages that Romanticism had once ascribed to nature, that erstwhile source of ultimate aesthetic truth. The enervated life of café society in fin de siècle Vienna signaled a culmination of the efforts launched by literary realism to make art reflect the industrial age, which had so dramatically altered the social make-up of European cities in the second half of the nineteenth century. Aided by its symbolic allure and the political economy of power, the city managed to contain extreme opposites simultaneously—the slums of the day laborer and the ballrooms of the nobility—as Walter Benjamin mused in his enigmatic essay "One-Way Street."

Just consider how, in the great modernist works of the twentieth century, subjective impressions quickly blossom into an objective expression of the urban spirit. The damp façades of Salzburg beneath the Kapuzinerberg and a deer's eye glimmering in the night is enough to make us feel at home in Georg Trakl's poem "Melancholie des Abends," proving that the city's mythology would be incomplete without his morphine-laced imagination. Amid the reeking Alexandria slums we intimate the portentous smiles of the young men for whom C. P. Cavafy chiseled eternal epitaphs in his poems, celebrating a fatalism of contacts never realized. Oriental sophistication found its memorial, too, in Lawrence Durrell's *Alexandria Quartet*, where we encounter not only Arabic chatter in impoverished souks, but also a proud patrician heritage and long centuries of tragic history. In the work of Fernando Pessõa, the fluttering raincoats of the lonely people who hurry past the artisan shops in Lisbon's Alfama district sketch, in the musty air of former grandeur, the portrait of a poet who celebrated his beloved city in a series of carefully chosen homonyms, the assumed names of imaginary poets writing different poems with one and the same soul. The poems Pessõa bequeathed to the twentieth century will live on long after the Portuguese folk dance, *fado*, has been done to death by the sterility of studio-produced "world beat" music.

The list could easily continue. The "magnetic fields" of the Parisian surrealists and the fearful liberty of its existentialists, consummated "to the last breath." Or consider the Roman novels of Alberto Moravia, which through the subtle use of middle-class civility explicate the way carnal desire in the Eternal

City clashes with the fear of scandal. And then there is Zagreb, bourgeois Zagreb, trying neurotically to substantiate the idea of its revered bard, Miroslav Krleža, that Central Europe's southern frontier begins on the terrace of the city's prestigious Hotel Esplanade. But there is also the Prague of Bohumil Hrabal's jovial beer taverns and Kafkaesque fog (or is that smog now?), as well as the Prague of Baroque sophistication that lives on in the novels of Milan Kundera. Or Belgrade, with its head in the clouds of a noble European tradition—represented by the Serbian surrealists and Vasko Popa—and with its geographical feet planted beneath the swinging lantern of a rowdy Balkan tavern. And Sarajevo, with its moral determination—despite the barbarism of the Serbian siege under indifferent Western eyes—to keep alive the best tradition of Izet Sarajlič's elegiac tributes, Abdulah Sidran's lyrical urban cantos, and Dževad Karahasan's poignant testimonies. Want more examples? How about the magic blush of the Buenos Aires suburbs in the *milongas* of Jorge Luis Borges, or St. Petersburg, as reflected in Anna Akhmatova's bitterly austere requiems or Joseph Brodsky's coldly beautiful, multifaceted poems? All right, let that be enough.

The point is this: what these cities have in common is not so much the cunning strategies of bankers, diplomats, soldiers, and merchants, but rather the work of their poets, writers, and artists, who over many decades created for each of them a specific symbolic iconography, through which, if only in the blink of an eye, all cities can be recognized. The poet possesses a deep intuitive feeling that the city limits demarcate the final frontier of the known world; that a particular city in some way *is* the entire world, an *imago mundi.* To be at home is to live in a city where earth meets sky and nothing is without a name; the city offers a primary and, therefore, a fundamental experience of space. The map of squares, alleys, streets, and corners in the provincial town where we were born or raised—the capital of "our" world, a pattern of the dwelling place of the gods—this map guides us relentlessly as we step onto the boulevards of foreign metropolises, driven by a yearning for "the other." But we can only sail from place to place, trying again and again to discern in "the other" something that is "the same." We seek, in fact, a primeval space, a place that has the meaning and weight of an archetype.

Ivan Cankar searched in vain for such an archetype in imperial Vienna. He found it only in Ljubljana. Sketches from the writer's "lonely, bitter youth" reveal his attachment to Vrhnika, his native marshland town southwest of Ljubljana, but it is the Slovene capital that commands most of his attention. The city acquires something of an aura in Cankar's work; it contains the possibility of collapse even as it spells out an ode of renewal. Cankar described this most explicitly in his short story "Kurent" (1909), which he dubbed an "ancient legend," suggesting a genre of integral mythic knowledge, although the story is marred by a sentimental tone:

> All blessings be yours, Ljubljana! Greater and more beautiful cities are there in the world, but none beneath the heavens is your equal! Hail, queen of happiness, mother of all delights, godmother of cheerful hours! A traveler with nine

burdens comes and greets you; by the time he bids you farewell, you have removed eight of his burdens.

The Distant Gaze

Cankar lived in cosmopolitan Vienna, but as an artist he was shaped by the cultural and political situation in provincial Ljubljana. Indeed, the totality of his
vision was founded on the habits of Slovene life. For Cankar, voluntary exile
was not so much a freely made decision to explore the new aesthetic styles in
literary Europe; more relevant was the fact that Vienna made possible a herme-
neutics of distance, both physical and mental. His creative demons were no
longer fettered by local community prejudices and there was no need to ask for-
giveness from the Slovene establishment; nor were any immediate privileges
offered such as had compromised the imagination of artists who stayed in
Ljubljana. Only distance made it possible for Cankar to give the necessary aesthetic twist to Slovene culture's craving for broader vistas and more generous
horizons. The distance of Vienna allowed Cankar to ponder the dialectics of
otherness and belonging and, along with this, the possibility for creating an un-
abashed encomium to his native land, which "stretches from the Styrian hills to
the steep Trieste coast, and from Mount Triglav to the Gorjanci Ridge." When
he returned to Ljubljana, the author of "Kurent" set about advancing the goals of
Slovene literary modernism: to bring the achievements of European expressive
form into correspondence with the idea of national identity.

In the modest history of national self-confidence, Slovene literary modernism, called in Slovene *moderna*, represents a crucial turning point and the first
cosmopolitan movement in the country. Never before had a loosely connected
group of artists, working in a wide range of disciplines and genres, put together
a program with such genuine (if perhaps, in retrospect, naïve) conviction—a
program where a sense of responsibility toward the national cultural tradition
would unite with individual talent. These artists opposed the moribund self-
satisfaction of the bourgeoisie so as to fashion at the beginning of the twentieth
century superb artworks that even today show the mark of originality. Such
originality seems particularly admirable when we consider that it had to contend
with the narrow-minded disdain of contemporaries. "Deadly boredom lies over
the whole city and its people," Cankar complained in a letter from Ljubljana to
his would-be Viennese bride.

At the core of this movement was something more than just a liberating focus on the nightingale-poet who must sing as God made him regardless of the
consequences; the movement was guided as well by a responsibility to expand
the symbolic boundaries, so as not only to offer new possibilities to the few chosen ones, as in Romanticism, but also to illuminate the existence of the entire
national collective. Beyond the liberation of the creative self from the shackles
of tradition, the works of the Slovene modernist movement reveal a mythologi-
cal nucleus in which "the spirit" of the tradition was preserved—but now re-

fashioned, revitalized, and made responsive to contemporary European art movements—while "the letter" of obsolete form was expelled. It is fair to say that the Slovene modernist movement presented an aesthetic blueprint for "the imagined community," as Benedict Anderson calls the tension between enduring myths, oral traditions, and archaic imagery on the one hand, and the contentious public reworking of this material on the other.

Solidarity and Autonomy

In this context, it would be a mistake to overlook the central image of Slovene modernism: the isolated individual, preferably an artist, who is misunderstood by the larger community precisely because he holds a critical mirror up to it. It would be very tempting, but wrong, to see in the cult of *the outsider*—exemplified by the main character in Cankar's 1901 novel *Strangers* [Tujci]—only a commonplace for the modern artist's despair. There is more to it. This focus on the outsider is a form of rejection of the status quo at that particular moment in Slovene history. The image of misunderstood artist is a literary response to bourgeois mediocrity, which drove Cankar to insist more than once that art "does not serve society but leads it."

Cankar was not alone in his efforts. Similar goals may be detected in the work of the Slovene impressionist painters whom local newspapers derisively dubbed "hayrackers"—the hayrack being an indelible feature on the Slovene landscape. For their first exhibition in Vienna—which Cankar praised—the painters Rihard Jakopič, Ivan Grohar, and Matija Jama used the adjective "Slovene" in a conscious and programmatic way. They understood that their personal idiom was fed by the underground currents of collective experience and thus saw past the blinkers of Slovene parochialism. Despite opposition at home, the Slovenian impressionists sent out precisely the same signal—about the need for a European expressive style and, simultaneously, responsibility toward the national community—that literary modernism was also trying to articulate.

The visionary concepts of the architect Jože Plečnik, contained in his never-realized project for a "Slovene Acropolis" on Ljubljana's Castle Hill, testify to this same spiritual program. The same can be said of his comprehensive redesign of Ljubljana, his native city, which, thanks to the architect's unique variety of classicism, underwent a transformation in organic modernity. Peter Krečič, in his book *Plečnik: The Complete Works* (1993), lays out good reasons for the architect's fame. Plečnik's ideas possess the same transhistorical impulse we find in Slovene literary modernism, intimating that the autonomy of creative talent does not need to be an obstacle to solidarity with the larger collective. In a dialectics of concealment and revelation, the critical examination of artworks which extend a handshake to the past in order to speak to the present, gives us a valuable perspective; it allows us to orient ourselves existentially, emotionally, and cognitively beyond life in the "perpetual now" imposed by the modern aesthetized world.

The Vicissitudes of Bilingualism

This kind of existential orientation is, at least for educated Slovenes, more or less self-evident. But of course, things that are self-evident to Slovenes remain obscure to any foreigner who comes into contact with work from this particular tradition. The juxtaposition of self-evidence and obscurity is, by and large, one of the structural features of the international public's response to the literatures of Central and Eastern Europe—not only Slovene, but also Slovak, Latvian, and Hungarian literatures, to name a few random examples.

I spent a good part of the year 1995 in Budapest. Hungary's renewed self-assurance in confronting post-communist problems had a galvanizing effect on my endeavors in barefoot anthropology—this, after all, requires a comparative approach. The Slovene collective imagination must dispense with the picture of impoverished Hungarians in smoke-belching Traband cars who each year jour-neyed to the sunny Adriatic beaches of Yugoslavia, a substitute for the capitalist West, which was virtually off-limits to tourists from Soviet Bloc countries; this once popular stereotype is marred by Slovenes' unwarranted sense of superiority. A quick look at the parallel historical development of Slovenia and Hungary will set the record straight.

Once one of the twin capitals of the Austro-Hungarian Empire, Budapest, with a population of two and a half million, extensive Western business invest-ments, and exuberant energy, not only has discovered the pleasures of the in-evitable Benetton stores and McDonald's restaurants; it has also enthusiastically rejuvenated its once glorious but for decades suppressed intellectual tradition. Perhaps the epitome of that earlier tradition is the famous Sunday Circle held in 1915 at Béla Balász's apartment, whose members included the young Arnold Hauser, Karl Mannheim, and Georg Lukács—thinkers without whom twentieth-century European cosmopolitanism would be distinctly poorer. True, these three representatives of the bygone Hungarian intellectual elite wrote more or less consistently in their adopted German; moreover, they all wrote theoretical works, which do not rely on the kind of intimate imagery that crops up when writing literary works in one's mother tongue. Theoretical discourse tends to employ the universal scientific method and a system of abstract concepts that are structurally identical around the globe; it thus offers relatively fair access to a competent expression in a "foreign" language. This is perhaps one reason why—apart from their professional excellence—a few Slovene intellectuals (notably, the internationally popular Lacanian philosopher Slavoj Žižek) have been able to penetrate the international arena somewhat more easily than literary writers, who bring with them the taxing totality of the existential world inherent to the mother tongue.

The functional bilingualism of Lukács, Mannheim, and Hauser was not an exception but the rule. This kind of cosmopolitan competence was a standard for the cream of the Hungarian cultural, business, and social elite, right up to World War I, as John Lukács reports in his book, *Budapest 1900*. And no wonder. Hungarians, like Slovenes, lived under the influence of German culture for many long centuries. Still, even here a huge difference persists between Slovenes and Hungarians. A thin layer of the bourgeoisie in Ljubljana, Celje, and Maribor communicated, for the most part, in German. But the Slovene cultural tradition as a whole has, alas, just a few genuinely bilingual intellectuals to show for it and hardly any truly bilingual writers.

Joseph Conrad, Vladimir Nabokov, Eugène Ionesco, Joseph Brodsky, and many other lesser-known modern writers have moved with ease through an atlas of various languages, entering worlds different from their own, which forced them to critically rethink the unquestioned customs of their homelands. A wide and open spirit allows for a continual, if demanding, process of comparison. Herein lies perhaps the greatest advantage of the cosmopolitan attitude, which, of course, is not necessarily linked to bilingualism as such. But the ability to express oneself in more than one language shows—in a figurative manner—that it is possible to avoid the bell jar of a single culture, which tries to homogenize its members, not only in an ethnic or national sense, but also in the habits of the heart and modes of thinking. In a homogeneous and monolingual culture, where there is no confrontation with different worlds, no heresy or dissent, no altered horizons of expectation—in such a culture many assumptions of existence are happily taken for granted. *If you haven't seen a castle, you'll be amazed by a pigsty,* says an old Slovene proverb, indicating that even peasant wisdom acknowledged the benefits of comparison. Bilingualism implies the internalization of the comparative perspective, which allows the individual to stand up to the Brave New World of the single truth.

In Slovene literary history, the associative chain of bilingualism reaches back to Anton Tomaž Linhart and his early play, the late-Baroque bourgeois drama *Miss Jenny Love* (1780). He wrote it in German and had it printed in the Bavarian town of Augsburg. But later, in accordance with the Enlightenment philosophy of turning to "the people," he exchanged German for his mother tongue and so wrote the first play ever in Slovene. After Linhart, many years passed before another writer emerged who could competently address the public in two languages. Not until the Romantic period do we come across another truly bilingual writer: Matija Čop, an erudite literary critic and philosopher of aesthetics, who, however, was not very prolific. The founder of modern Slovene poetry, France Prešeren, was genuinely bilingual. As a political statement against Austria's domination of the Slovene people, however, he refused, by and large, to write his poems in German.

Perhaps it becomes a little easier to understand Ivan Cankar in the light of such linguistic solitude—not the physical state of not having other people around, but the metaphysical situation in which others do not understand what are you saying. Vienna, the capital of "nervous splendor," as historian Frederic Morton aptly describes the city, was Cankar's home for an entire decade. But (here I chip away at an entrenched national myth) he lived there not as a respected writer from one of the more than thirty nations under the rule of the Imperial and Royal House of Habsburg. Instead, wrapped in a cloak of anonymity, he never met his famous Viennese contemporaries; he "merely" read their

works. Cankar never managed to establish any fruitful personal contacts with
the leading minds of his day; torn between depression and creative fever, he
holed up in a miserable rented room. What saved him was devotion to his work,
which was intended for his compatriots, the readers who lived some two hundred and fifty miles away across the Alps.

The Weather Station at the End of the World

But just imagine it! This, after all, was fin de siècle Vienna, an imaginary museum of art nouveau style, where Leon Trotsky, then a Russian émigré and later
the architect of permanent proletarian revolution, played chess in glamorous
Café Central with Viktor Adler, the leader of Austrian social democracy whose
political ideas had such a decisive influence on Cankar. Cankar himself, meanwhile, was reading newspapers in the dingy Beethoven Coffeehouse, frequented
mainly by malnourished students. This, after all, was self-assured Vienna, where
the gnomic propositions of Ludwig Wittgenstein coexisted with Sigmund
Freud's analysis of ego; gorgeous Vienna, where the architectural historicism of
Otto Wagner shook hands with the decadent beauty of the paintings of Gustav
Klimt; frenzied Vienna, where Arthur Schnitzler's erotic anxiety could not but
encounter the tragic sublimation of instincts in the work of Hugo von Hof-
mannsthal—Vienna, capital of the waltz, a dance that, under the stinging pen of
Karl Kraus, quite appropriately turned into a *danse macabre.*

It was in such a Vienna that Cankar produced a string of important literary
works, which remain essential even today for Slovenes' self-understanding.
Cankar's damaged, embittered, and déclassé characters suggest that he almost
certainly found Vienna to be a kind of "weather station at the end of the world,"
as Kraus sarcastically put it. Cankar naturally used German as his public language in Vienna. For two years, he even contributed political columns to the
Viennese weekly *Die Süden*, the newsletter *Die Information*, and the newspaper
Die Arbeiter. But it would never occur—rightly—to any literary historian to
interpret these quickly abandoned attempts as evidence of bilingual creativity. If
bilingualism, at least in part, opens up mechanisms of engagement in a larger
cross-cultural context, then we must admit that Slovene writers have not been
internationally acknowledged.

The presence of Slovenes in the larger cultural currents of Europe does not
even take the sort of mediated form we find in the letter of praise Thomas Mann
sent to Dezso Kosztolányi, a highly respected Hungarian writer, after reading his
novel *Darker Muses* (1922): "This is an amazingly fine novel, which reveals an
individual originality that can move mankind." Notice that this was a personal
contact between two modernists, linked by mutual literary respect and the ethics
of social distinction. The literary patriarch of Europe was giving recognition to
an internationally less famous, though nationally celebrated author. For Mann to
comment at all on Kosztolányi's artistic abilities, he had to be familiar with his
work in the first place. How far removed was Cankar from this kind of recogni-

tion! If one looks really hard, then there is a letter from Eugenio Montale, one of the major Italian poets of the twentieth century, in which he admiringly tells his mentor, Bobi Bazlen, that Ivan Cankar is "a giant of European literature." But alas, this letter has for too long gathered archival dust to have any mitigating effect on Cankar's anonymity in the larger cosmos of European literary signs.

A couple more examples present themselves for our comparison: the experimental methods of the Hungarian visual artist László Moholy-Nagy helped articulate the avant-garde aesthetics of the Bauhaus; the Slovene painter Avgust Černigoj, by contrast, studied only for a short time under the international aegis of the Bauhaus, though with far-reaching consequences for Slovene constructivism. The Budapest psychoanalyst and art collector Szandor Ferenczi personally assisted Freud in his work; by contrast, Freud could keep an anonymous Slovene patient from Trieste on his couch for only a few sessions before throwing up his hands in despair over the man's alleged lack of cooperation—today, this self-involved man exists only in a footnote to Freud's collected works. Long is the history of Slovene marginality on the European scene.

Budapest: A Central European Forum

A provisional comparison of the neighboring Slovene and Hungarian traditions reveals even deeper social-historical differences. With its narrow streets crammed beneath Ljubljana Castle, where the gilded luxury of the Spanheim dukes flaked off centuries ago, with just a few bourgeois mansions, and with the modesty of an Austrian provincial seat, Ljubljana has little in common with Budapest, even at first glance. The charm of decay and, paradoxically, selective urban renovation is today transforming the Hungarian capital into an attractive city with significant fin de siècle architecture and a faded imperial grandeur that rivals Vienna's.

The subdued beauty of Ljubljana's red-tile roofs, a few wonderful squares, its three-pronged bridge, and the languid curves of the river embankment have not yet penetrated the consciousness of international travelers, let alone the global film industry. On the other hand, the architectural shape of Budapest was made famous in Ernst Lubitsch's 1940 film *The Shop Around the Corner,* when he set an enchanting love story between James Stewart and Margaret Sullivan on the wide boulevards of bourgeois Pest and aristocratic Buda. No need to dwell on the little-known fact that for the crowd scenes in Madonna's 1996 film *Evita,* director Alan Parker used Budapest as a stand-in for Buenos Aires. Budapest's involvement with American film, in fact, begins decades earlier when many Hungarian artists, fleeing the Nazis, emigrated to Hollywood in the 1930s and 1940s. As for Slovenes in Hollywood, meticulous historical research has turned up only a few stagehands and support personnel.

But even when we set aside the great names of the past, it becomes even harder to ignore the differences between the two cities today. Budapest's former cosmopolitan character has been reinvigorated by international institutions that serve as a magnet for creative intellect from all over the region and beyond. Consider, for example, the Central European University, the brainchild of Hungarian American philanthropist George Soros; the Cold War Archives of Radio Free Europe and Radio Liberty, which once broadcast programs to countries behind the Iron Curtain; the Collegium Budapest–Institute for Advanced Study, which, among other things, encourages international scholars and artists to pursue long-term collaborative projects with local partners; and the Open Media Research Institute, where an international group of scholars is studying the regional mass media during the post-communist "transition." Two English-language weeklies and a thick telephone directory of services offered in English; a multitude of international businessmen, journalists, artists, and professors; scholarly journals in English, such as *The New Hungarian Quarterly,* which has been publishing for a number of years, and the more recent *Budapest Review of Books,* where foreigners can learn about the achievements of Hungarian intellectual production; the colorful commotion on Váci Street, the main tourist artery, where you are likely to hear not only German and Ukrainian, but also Arabic and Yoruba—all this cultural and social hubbub very palpably leaves the impression that Budapest, which among other things can boast having the first electric subway on the continent (dating from 1896), is returning to the very center of European cultural life, a position it occupied before the fall of the Habsburgs.

No nostalgic Pollyanna can bring back la belle époque; the Hungarians seem well aware of this. They understand that their national identity will be strengthened only by a self-assured confrontation with all that is foreign, other, and different. As a former imperial power, the Hungarians, of course, have vast experience with more or less open repression of other nations, but they also know what uneasy coexistence is like. Perhaps this is why post-communist Hungary—reinforced by the return of the intellectual and economic émigré community—is rushing to set up new economic, cultural, and academic institutions, housed in the old mansions that line the avenues patterned on Vienna's grand Ringstrasse.

These institutions aim to prepare the Hungarian nation for the challenges of the twenty-first century and possibly help it weather the deep crisis of transition. The essential social challenge of post-communism is, above all, to negotiate a balance that can preserve the cultural uniqueness of the national identity without retreating into dangerous isolation and shutting out the sometimes coercive influx of foreign capital, ideas, and knowledge. This politics of balance derives from a conviction that domestic wisdom will likely be enhanced if it is exposed to unending dialogue, fostering an awareness that the community's greater cultural growth needs to be viewed as a two-way street, as part of the give-and-take of international communication.

A Two-Way Street

A reader by vocation and profession, I visited the bookstores of Budapest religiously during my stay there. With both admiration and frustration I took from the shelves both classic and current Hungarian authors in English, German, and French translations. Clearly, the descendents of the nomadic Huns understand the principle of the two-way street. I am not just talking about internationally recognized authors like the novelist Péter Esterházy, the essayist Georgy Konrád, or the prose writers Péter Nádas and Imre Kertesz; they have regular publishers in the West. Hungarians know that, when it comes to making potential readers familiar with their national identity—which exists, linguistically, on a lonely Finno-Ugric island amidst a sea of Slavs—a certain amount of orchestration is required. So, at least until recently, Hungarian publishing companies would themselves print translations of nationally important authors. It has been a wise strategy. Many foreigners who come to Budapest want to learn not only about internationally acclaimed writers, but also about the local cultural scene. Hungarian intellectuals, apparently, want to do more than simply recite the annals of their centuries-long involvement with Western Christianity and Europe—which is often the be-all and end-all in the debates of post-communist Slovene culturati.

It is hardly a coincidence that Endre Ady, the most famous Hungarian poet of the early twentieth century, in the poem that stands as a programmatic epigraph to his *New Poems* (1906), wrote lines in which his personal ambition is closely tied to the ambitions of the national collective: "I shall cross at Dévény / with new poems for new times." Dévény is the westernmost Hungarian village on the Danube, the point where the river enters traditionally Hungarian territory. As such, Dévény symbolizes the threshold of the European West, with which Hungarian intellectuals and writers actively collaborated. Even the name of the literary journal *Nyugat* (West), founded in 1908 in the wake of an explosion in Ady's popularity, bespeaks the Hungarian intellectual elite's orientation toward urban sensibilities and cosmopolitan attitudes.

Slovenes face a number of obstacles when they try to participate actively in the international flow of ideas and metaphors. To begin with, there is their history of recent confinement beneath the umbrella of Yugoslav culture, which I discussed elsewhere in this book. Moreover, the Slovene émigré communities in North and South America and Western Europe have, sadly, played only a negligible role in promoting Slovene culture internationally—in contrast with the Czech, Romanian, Hungarian, and Polish diasporas, which have nurtured a number of strong individuals and cultural institutions, from literary reviews to scholarly institutions and publishing houses. Nevertheless, Tomaž Šalamun is not the only figure in contemporary Slovene literature who managed to overcome such limitations; the novelist and essayist Drago Jančar, too, has transcended the boundaries of his mother tongue, making successful forays on the international literary scene. In 1996, he presented his dark aesthetic vision to the parliament of Austria, an institution that Ivan Cankar, despite his ten-year residence in Vienna, could only view from the outside. A participant in many European intellectual forums, Jančar shares with other well-known writers from "the Other Europe" a powerful drive to express, as he says, "the unrest of history." Translations of Jančar's works have appeared both as individual books and in numerous anthologies and journals, spreading his art throughout the world, though Europe remains his principal turf. Jančar's creative energy has manifested itself in numerous collections of political essays and cultural meditations, plays and film scenarios, novels and short stories. Slovenes have not had such a multifaceted and internationally successful writer at least since Ivan Cankar. But even Cankar, with only a few Croatian and Czech translations published during his lifetime, had a much more limited reach. Jančar, not unlike Cankar, finds inspiration in the violence of historical caprice that takes place beneath the dark clouds of Central Europe's peculiar "meteorological phenomenon"—as Austrian writer Peter Handke once ridiculed the search for meaning in this part of the world. Despite the obstacles that come with writing in the language of a small nation, Jančar's works today reach far beyond the boundaries of the former Habsburg dominions.

With an express sense of responsibility to the national culture, Jančar represents the kind of writer who understands that *homo poeticus* does not reside only in the rarefied altitudes of aesthetic play. Jančar walks the tightrope between "yogi" and "commissar," oscillating between artistic self-exploration and political engagement, all the better to capture the affairs of everyday life. His writings spring from a passionate anxiety about the psychological and physical damage that recent centuries have inflicted on Slovene collective life. With his stylized illumination of time and place as we live it, Jančar's voice offers something essential to the public, something that is missing from many newspaper commentaries: his own vulnerable being, his righteous anger, and the pulse of his anxious self.

In the 1970s, Jančar spent a few months in a Yugoslav jail. He was convicted of possessing "enemy propaganda," specifically, prohibited books about and by Slovene political emigrants. His time in prison earned him added moral credibility. But more important than any halo of anticommunist dissidence is Jančar's capacity for literary empathy, which allows him to speak with both the voice of a seer and a reporter's attention to detail. Jančar thus pulls the carpet out from under the clay feet of aestheticist theory. In his novel *Northern Lights* [Severni sij] (1980), the metaphor of the aurora borealis, which in folk tradition augurs evil changes, shoots out from a very real "extra-textual" fabric, namely, the social, political, and cultural disputes between German and Slovene nationalists in a small Slovene town just before the outbreak of World War II. This celestial metaphor shines with the glare of intertribal conflict, something that is no less human than the need for shelter and that has been with us ever since war broke out between Sparta and Athens.

Because Jančar's literary works unite in a coherent way local cultural tradition and individual talent, I see his international success, alongside Šalamun's, as paving the way for a new generation of Slovene writers. They should find the going a little easier, once they tear themselves away from the domestic shores and begin to navigate the choppy cosmopolitan waters. And, like Jančar and Šalamun, they should be able to demonstrate on the evidence of their work that the world's literary map cannot be complete until the blank spot of Slovenia is filled.

Chapter 4

Europe without Europeans

The Political Economy of Insecurity

It is a hot summer afternoon and crowds of tourists seek shade in the shining streets of the Umbrian town of Assisi. The stroller I push holds a thirsty one-year-old baby, my five-year-old daughter wants a sandwich, and my three-year-old son is pleading to get a closer look at the dragon on the door handle of the Saint Francis Hotel. So our family decides to make a stop in the hotel's lobby. Sweaty, in khaki shorts, laden with swollen bags of diapers and picture books, and chattering excitedly, we make our way past the solemn modernistic paintings on the walls, the bored receptionist, and the temptingly luxurious armchairs. Surprisingly gentle music can be heard coming from invisible speakers. Although we do nothing but walk through the lobby and settle on the terrace, I am suddenly overcome by a familiar feeling of uneasiness.

It is the same uneasiness I regularly experience in luxury hotels in Western Europe and the United States: mild anxiety and vague trepidation, a fear that the porter might mercilessly throw me out of the hotel should I make a single wrong step or do anything that could fatally expose the fact that I am unfamiliar with the proper code of communication and lack an inherent self-confidence—distinctive characteristics of people who know their place in the world. While it may not be immediately obvious that I am an "Easterner," "Slav," or someone from "the Balkans," and my physiognomy may not say much about my ethnic origin, the way I cross the parquet floor nonetheless exposes me. The political economy of insecurity manifests itself in the most minuscule gestures and facial expressions. My cautious manner betrays not only the experience of socialist poverty which accompanied my student hitch-hiking trips to Western Europe, but, above all, a bitter awareness that I possess a hidden, unrecognizable identity. This is not the same as being unnoticed. Rather, it comes from a lack of context, the absence of any web of emblematic cultural and psychological signs that would allow a person to determine my region of origin. I have a feeling that I owe something to somebody, that my place is not in the parlor, idly flipping through the pages of today's *L'Espresso* or *International Herald Tribune.* Instead, my place—for which I am supposed to feel grateful—is at best somewhere outside, on the margins of the public space of acceptable society, on the terrace, not quite in the street but certainly not in the air-conditioned luxury reserved for the chosen ones. And my sense is that this is not just my own personal experience whispering in my ear, but also the historical—and surely problematic—collective narrative of the region and nation to which I belong.

My American wife is not hampered by these mental obstacles. In principle, all hotels the world over are the same for her: they serve travelers, supplying them with food, drink, safety, the familiarity of language and accommodations, and perhaps even enjoyable company. Granted, my frustrating feeling of unease may derive from personal psychological idiosyncrasies. I would be hard-pressed, however, to believe that this feeling is not hinged, too, on the legacy of communism as a collective environment of customs and styles of behavior, as well as the residue of a social division that sets a privileged party hierarchy apart from the anonymous "working class." Moreover, I am increasingly convinced that my insecurity is also rooted in the no less important fact that the very name of my country, when mentioned in everyday conversation (including in that particular hotel lobby, and in a neighboring country, to boot!), still elicits incomprehensive looks at best, and suspicious or even scornful reactions at worst. As a category of ordinary public discourse in the "developed democracies" of the West, Slovenia, along with most of Eastern and Central Europe, cannot be found in the directory of recognizable topographies, and certainly not on the list of meaningful social references. Since Slovenia has not been domesticated as part of the public discourse, it cannot expect to be considered civilized. It is still too unknown, too foreign, too different.

Europe versus the "Other Europe"

Both the social legacy of communism and the cultural heritage of the "Other Europe"—as Czesław Miłosz once aptly labeled the lands east of the now-fallen iron curtain—continue to represent a vague disturbance or incomprehensible murmur in European discourse. And it is precisely Europe—as a civilizational habitus—that forms the framework in which the countries of the continent's eastern half project their political and emotional aspirations. Europe is the standard they use to measure the depth of their collective pain, yet they are not a self-evident and integral part of it. We, who come from a region of blurs on the map, the birthplace of tribal consciousness and fanatic hatred, the site of Ottoman backwardness and Byzantine corruption, the home of turbulent primitive passions and gripping mythical stories—we present a disturbing figure wherever we turn up.

And no wonder. Western Europe is to an overwhelming degree engaged in the art of navel-gazing. It is obsessed with itself. Not very long ago, in 1993, Western Europe made it known *urbi et orbi* that it shamelessly, indeed grotesquely, prefers to give pride of place to Maastricht rather than Sarajevo, choosing to focus on its own internal integration rather than on the largest geopolitical earthquake on the continent in half a century. Though I might be rationalizing things in retrospect, I am sure that such a choice of priorities was not a coincidence, much less the result of some "technicality." In my opinion, it was the consequence of reasoning within a politically flawed and strategically limited frame. In keeping with the European Union's own genesis, this perspective—which represents that of Western Europe in general—has a specific kind of logic. Today, this logic is highly problematic.

The Maastricht Treaty, with its blueprint for monetary union and its major overhaul of the 1957 Treaty of Rome, which established the precursor to the contemporary European Union, is a metaphor of the E.U.'s priorities. It showed that West European countries preferred to focus on their own integration process—as if the process was itself the goal and not merely the means to a higher form of political order. As such, it functions in accordance with a specific vision of the future that has considerable difficulty accepting the reality of Eastern and Central Europe, the Balkans, and the Baltics. It looks with suspicion on all these strange languages, all these small new countries ("Listen, who would be able to name them all!" the renowned German poet and cultural critic Hans Magnus Enzensberger exclaimed in despair in the early 1990s) with their funny songs and strange customs, a fanatic sparkle in their eyes, and a fatalistic delight in inconsequential discussions, atavistic impulses, and general confusion. In this context, the emphasis on the Maastricht agreement suggested that the E.U. considered it necessary—against the backdrop of burning Balkan villages and towns—to deal primarily with its own integration, in other words, to clean its own house regardless of what was happening right outside. One tries to understand this rationally, of course, but it is impossible to accept morally. It is like trying to accept the fact that business must go on as usual even when someone in the family is very sick. Family members can express emphatic solidarity and, at least in principle, identify with those who belong to its fold; such emphatic solidarity can extend to members of the same clan or community. Anthropological theory tells us that the differentiating traits between groups are arbitrary only in kind; they are not arbitrary in the structural function of ties that provide the common code by which group members recognize each other. Common sense suggests that our sense of obligation to help others in need varies depending on the nature of our relationship to them—whether, for example, these others are family members, friends, or fellow citizens.

Common sense cannot be altered overnight. It may very well be true that more than a decade has passed since communism crumbled as a political system. But a decade in which public euphoria has been increasingly replaced by skeptical and, more often than not, outright negative attitudes toward the peoples, habits, expectations, and mores of former communist lands is certainly not a sufficient period of time to permit a radical, more inclusive reorientation of the West European focus.

Western Europe, it seems to me, continues to be a "family apart" from the rest of the continent despite the grand expansion of European Union in 2004. In this regard, I would like to discuss briefly three aspects of the modern construction of Europe that have come to represent the main pillars of the post–World War II European order. Because these pillars are inherently flawed, Europe cannot hope to foster "ever closer union" without seriously rethinking them. I have in mind the following three problems: first, the *negative articulation* of Europe; second, *economism* as Europe's founding myth; and third, *the feeble design of the common mental framework*. Without making any attempt at a comprehensive picture, I will limit myself to three main propositions: a defense of *a more inclusive understanding of Europe,* which must refuse any inclination to ignore the post-communist countries; a call for *culturally conditioning the master narrative* in order to reduce, if not displace, its dependence on the utilitarian philosophy of the free market; and a reminder of *the intrinsic difficulty of constructing a template* for a common European identity.

Over the past fifty years, Western Europe has been increasingly able to usurp the historical idea of Europe as a whole by means of the political and cultural institutions of the Cold War. A network of procedures, designed to establish and evaluate standards of appropriate conduct, refers to the heritage of the Enlightenment and the ethics of professional responsibility in all discussions about political cooperation and economic and legal integration. These procedures, however, have tacitly enhanced the exclusive nature of the European idea. Such excusivism can be seen, for example, in Western Europe's persistently negative stance towards Muslims—ever since the Crusades—as a symbol for all that is "foreign," for all that stands outside European civilization, as Tomaž Mastnak brilliantly demonstrates in his *Crusading Peace: Christendom, the Muslim World, and Western Political Order.* I do not intend to speak here about the special case of Islam in Europe, though certainly that was one of the key factors behind Western Europe's passivity in regard to the Balkan crisis and the nearly successful genocide of the Bosnian Muslims. Muslims are but a painfully evident metaphor for something that cannot easily be integrated—without involving large conceptual problems—into the symbolic context of the European habitus, which is spontaneously understood as Christian by many of the peoples of Western Europe. Muslims serve as a provisional, although not mistaken, illustration of the element of foreignness. In the 1990s, this foreign element was represented (to a different degree of acceptability) by the post-communist lands. The predominant discourse that gives rise to such exclusivity is, of course, not fixed. But regardless of its various historical configurations, it derives from the fact that modern "Europeanism" as a *forma mentis* was shaped during the Cold War.

For this reason, the parameters of selection that govern the primary, if not all, spheres of life in Western Europe, are still essentially marked by the binary assumption "us" versus "them," as David Kideckel argues in a 1994 essay, "Us and Them: Concepts of East and West in the East European Transition." I am not saying that there is only one sort of public rhetoric. A plurality of views occurs within this presumed framework, which is more or less widely accepted among both the elites and the general public. Assimilated into the horizon of expectations, it is part and parcel of the interpretive models that attempt, with difficulty, to account for the changing European map—not only the geopolitical map, but also Europe's cognitive mapping. Such cognitive mapping continues to rely on well-worn, persistent clichés. And what could be more persistent than the stereotype of Eastern Europe as the Other Europe, a place inhabited by shabby citizens and corrupt psychopaths, or potentially dangerous beggars who have little regard for the rules of common decency and law-abiding conduct?

Indeed, it is not excessive to argue that, even before it has attained any positive unified substance in economic, political, cultural, and social terms, modern Europe as a mental space has already been negatively articulated. This negativity came out of a publicly and institutionally entrenched need to contain the common enemy on the other side of the Iron Curtain. The homogenization of Western Europe could take place only by negation: not by affirming what it is, but by determining its boundaries through a definition of what it is not. The physicality of the boundary between "the Free World" and "the Evil Empire" of communism, with its walls, barbed wires, mine fields, and trigger-happy guards, only strengthened and legitimized Europe's fearful asymmetry. In such a context, the mental structure of European identity remained determined by the "foreign" element, damaged and damaging.

When Western Europe, after the devastation of World War II, was struggling to get back on its feet and consolidate itself, philosophical notions and cultural images were not enough. The representation of "Europeanism" had to be grounded in an impersonal logic of self-propelling principles able to provide, at first sight, a dividing line on the most tangible, most direct and, thus, most accessible level. The gospel of the accumulation of capital, that is to say, the procedures of trade and business conduct established by the Marshall Plan and the Organization for European Economic Cooperation (OEEC) and articulated not long after the World War II, played a major unifying role in Western Europe. These economic plans came to be accepted as the repositories of formative, binding, and functional values. Founded more on the developed tradition of industrial capitalism than the achievements of social democracy, these values have been assimilated in the daily habits of West European citizens. Thus, a general standard was shaped against which any attempt to shift the social, moral, aesthetic, and ideological boundaries is seen as deviant or subversive.

Western Europe as the vehicle of these values has begun to translate them into a series of institutions and procedures intended to ensure their survival and protect the quality of life of all who honor and uphold them. The European Union, while certainly not the only transnational body on the continent, surely deserves to be seen as the preeminent project in which European aspirations to commonality are embedded. It is through the E.U. that West European countries participate in this formidable task: through apparently neutral bureaucratic methods, a standard of conduct and the norms of a conceptual and imaginative appropriation of experience are increasingly transposed into a growing body of formal regulations and procedural rules. These regulations are invested with the belief that they guarantee not only a particular way of doing business and conducting political, economic, and social affairs within and between member states, but also that they provide transcendental meaning to the norms and values they advance. In this regard, the triumph of capitalism and democracy after the "Velvet Revolutions" of Central and Eastern Europe in 1989 was seen as a confirmation of the universal status these norms and values seemingly possess.

Reconstructing Europeanism?

More than ten years after the Velvet Revolutions and the violent breakup of Yugoslavia, however, it has become clear that unquestioned coordination between "European" symbolic, moral, political, and social values, on one hand, and "European" capitalism, on the other, is no longer tenable. A Pandora's box was opened after the fall of the Berlin Wall and it cannot be closed up again. As the eastern part of the continent witnesses the rise of fanatic nationalism and the birth of many new countries based on old (though not always discernible) ethnic traditions, Western Europe turns a blind eye to the return of a suppressed history, convinced that the "spring of nations" was something that happened long ago. It seems that the painful history of nineteenth century—the unification of the German Länder, the stitching together of the Italian provinces ("We have Italy, now we need Italians!" Massimo D'Azeglio notoriously exclaimed), and the brutal ethnic homogenization carried out by the French state—is nowadays completely forgotten. If these past nationalist movements had more clearly been integrated into the symbolic horizon of Europe, perhaps today one would not so easily get the impression that, whereas nationalism in the bigger countries is legitimate, nationalism in the new, smaller countries inevitably sets off alarm bells. In order for European integration to begin, it was imperative that the nationalist history of Western Europe be suppressed. Thus, erstwhile nationalistic countries have become enthusiastic Europeans under the cover of economic prosperity and a consensus on the inevitable progress of the "common market." It was precisely in an effort to facilitate this progress, that Winston Churchill, in a famous speech at Zurich University in 1946, based the reconstruction of the European family on a prospective partnership between France and Germany.

France and Germany—which together represent the leading force for European integration today and, indeed, have a great deal invested in the existence of a strong Europe (although for different reasons)—have more or less buried their nationalist animosities by facing the demons of their own totalitarian history (the Vichy regime, the Third Reich). While their visions of the E.U.'s future structure may differ, based as they are on the countries' specific histories (the French republican tradition of a strong state and the German development of constitutional checks designed to preclude the possibility of another Holocaust), we nevertheless can discern a common denominator in all their essential European efforts, namely, the nationalism of a fat purse.

Do not misunderstand me. There is no doubt that the historical reconciliation between these two traditional adversaries represents a significant achievement of political deliberation and is worthy of profound respect. But we would be misguided not to recognize the primacy of economic logic as the basis for this reconciliation. It was, after all, the economic integration of Western Europe that was the truly essential factor in Jean Monnet's and Robert Schumann's original idea. The political goal was to forever prevent Germany from building a war machine with the resources of mining and heavy industry in Saar and Ruhr valleys. A lasting peace between traditionally hostile countries could be achieved so long as any potential war is not only conceptually incomprehensible but also economically impractical. The forerunner of the E.U., the European Coal and Steel Community (ECSC), which was established in 1951 in Paris by six signatory countries, became the first truly supranational organization in postwar Europe to have teeth, regulating the production of coal, steel, and iron ore. The master narrative on which the legitimacy of postwar Europe rests was devised in order to prevent any new catastrophic breakouts of imperial chauvinism and ethnic megalomania, the past scars of which needed a long time to heal. Economic resources were used to further the process of unification in order to achieve a political goal, namely, the renunciation of force in resolving disputes among members of the Union.

The creation of a European "community of peace" is predicated, then, on a pragmatic consideration, which, however, demands to be teleologically justified. The telos of peace as the supreme value provides the irrefutable language of necessity embedded in the foundations of European unification. Such unification is required for the liberalization of the intra-European market, reinforcement of habits of institutional cooperation, and reduction of cultural and societal mistrust among the members. Economic integration would provide a sense of interdependence among the peoples, and this was supposed to keep the psychology of fear at bay and so, hopefully, eradicate the breeding ground for the kind of catastrophe that had devastated Warsaw, Berlin, Budapest, and Leningrad. Impediments to global trade and the free flow of capital were to be abolished and, in this way, international conflicts would eventually cease. This mantra, though not necessarily heard every day, functions as an unquestioned assumption behind every argument promoting "Europeanism." The less one hears it, the more effective it is.

The technocratic discourse of the E.U. fails, then, to set forth any comprehensive, albeit idealistic, vision that might give people direction and meaning beyond the realm of the mundane. Instead, it derives from a conviction that all visions are corrupt; one need only ensure the conditions for free trade, and all the rest will follow. Here, and here alone, has Europe managed to amalgamate irreconcilable differences. I am reminded of Blaise Pascal's observation that the most important thing in the development of faith is exterior form: if a set prayer, for example, is repeated daily as part of a ritual, religious sentiment will follow spontaneously.

One can see the same principle at work in the discourse of E.U. experts, now linked to the perverted latter-day Cartesianism "I shop, therefore I am." At a time when one ostensibly revolutionary idea after another has collapsed, producing immense suffering in its wake, many pundits continue to recite the mantra of the "invisible hand of the market." But this merely obscures the fact that, if the hand of the market must remain invisible, it is only because it extends its middle finger. At a time of vast inequities in wealth and opportunity, relentless degradation of the environment, and proliferating outlets of consumerist indulgence, which have all but displaced any sense of responsible citizenship, great numbers of self-styled political realists continue to entertain the exclusivist illusions of Western Europe and of the E.U. as the one and only site of relevance.

Instead of radically reconsidering the continent's changed cultural, moral, political, and economic terrain following the tumultuous collapse of communist *anciens régimes,* the E.U. engine, alas, merely kept on rambling along tracks that had been laid out for it before anyone could have imagined the possibility of an undivided Europe. Technologically advanced, economically dynamic, and rapidly integrating the western half of the continent, the E.U. miserably failed in recognizing the historic opportunity it was offered. "We fiddled when Sarajevo burned," Timothy Garton Ash pointedly laments in his *History of the Present.* By "we" he means, of course, Western Europe.

What exactly was the missed opportunity? Above all, it was a chance for the E.U. to liberate itself from the heritage of the Cold War. Instead, Western Europe maintained the polarization by other means: now, instead of seeing them as the enemy, the E.U. viewed the countries that had freed themselves from the communist straightjacket as poor relatives with unrealistic ambitions and a childish wish to imitate the West. To the extent that the Cold War was fought on the basis of competing ideological claims and belief systems—that is, in thinly veiled metaphysical terms—the E.U. has remained a willing prisoner of its own received wisdom. In this respect, it could do nothing but see itself as the site of a unique civilization representing the ultimate horizon of universal aspirations, a civilization of superior values and the ultimate guarantee of their survival.

For the political elites of the post-communist countries, crowding in the waiting room of this contradictory club, the understanding of the E.U. as a place of superior standards, norms, and values in all walks of life has undoubtedly possessed great mobilizing power. This was not a question of selective rational deliberation but, rather, a comprehensive idea that presented the E.U. as a promise of happiness and the alleviation of all tensions—an Arcadia from which the peoples of the East had been expelled at the onset of communism; after the revolutions of 1989, they could simply return to their "natural" habitat. It is thus no coincidence that the "return to Europe" represented one of the very few clearly identifiable rallying cries in Central and Eastern Europe in the 1990s. This slogan was felt as genuine in various public circles and enjoyed wide support among the people in general, and not only among the post-communist elites, who, however, quickly discovered (regardless of whether they leaned left or right) that symbolism doesn't get you very far. In countries where communism had preached only absolute dichotomies, "Europe" now meant the embodiment of beauty, truth, and justice. Before long, the public discourse of Eastern and Central Europe had placed "Europe" on a pedestal as a metaphysical idea, something sacred and beyond all doubt.

Europe, then, was a privilege. No privilege, however, can survive its practical universalization. From this particular point of view, it is not surprising—though it is unacceptable for me—that in contemporary debates about what privilege it is we are really talking about, the traditionally overlooked part of Europe is, in fact, omitted. The entire post-communist world is present in these debates only through its absence. Let me state this clearly: the post-communist world is not an active participant in these debates, that is, it is excluded from any possibility of substantially influencing the outcome of negotiations on the emerging European political, cultural, and economic identity in the twenty-first century. Regardless of differences in the achieved forms of democratic order and market efficiency, the state of human rights, and the established institutions of the rule of law, as exhibited today by the countries aspiring to join the E.U., it is safe to say that the least common denominator they share is a consensus about the need to reduce the complex processes of integration. This means reduction to the instrumental-pragmatic dimension. The adoption of the huge corpus of the *acquis communautaire* and its integration into individual national legislation in post-communist countries is generally understood as a formal, technical obligation and less as a central political mechanism of rearranging the fundamental relations not only between the state and the civil society, but also between the state and existing cultural, ethnic, and historical identifications.

In this light, we need to consider possibilities for constructing a common template for an inclusive European identity that will have wide public appeal. Here, too, Western Europe's preconceived notions and excessive reliance on the integrating effects of "economism" and nothing else tend to undermine, rather than invite, the construction of a viable shared master narrative. Moreover, the dominance of the E.U.'s economic aspect continues exactly to the extent to which comprehensive and rationally organized attempts to formulate a "common mental framework" for the E.U. are doomed to failure. Such joint projects as the "Cultural Capital of Europe" program, which fosters mutual understanding between European nations; the Erasmus, Socrates, and Tempus scholarships, which are designed to encourage the sharing of scientific research; international human rights workshops; and support for efforts to build a democratic mentality in the public at large—all these and many other welcome forms of European cooperation will hang in a limbo of limited engagement if they are not anchored to a common grand narrative.

What, exactly, do I mean by this? What I have in mind is a substantial imaginative framework of general identification, material for "common dreams" that can give all the citizens of Europe a certain minimum of existential meaning and emotional density, through which we recognize a commitment to something that transcends us as individuals with particular identities. I realize, of course, that such a construction is idealistic, hinged as it is on a search for balance between ethnic and cultural traditions on the one hand, and loyalty to a supranational, overarching cultural habitus on the other. Yet I cannot bring myself to believe that the reciprocity of horizontal transactions that would give each member equal say in the affairs of the whole can be established without mutual acceptance of a publicly shared sphere within which such reciprocity can take place.

My own experience, however, along with a consideration of the genesis of national identification as the strongest form of modern collective allegiance, tells me that Europeanism cannot be an effective unifying narrative unless it consciously and systematically draws from the heritage of all European nations. As such, Europeanism would have to meet several demanding standards. It would have to include cross-generational continuity, perpetuated by a common cultural amalgamation of distinct ethnic traditions and reinforced by shared memory and the expectation of a common future, as Dominique Moisi points out in the essay "Dreaming of Europe." In other words, Europeanism would need to provide a symbolic order wherein a centripetal force might be able to counteract—though by no means abolish—the centrifugal forces of primary identification that one feels as a Pole, German, Catalan, Croatian, Scot, or Italian. The emotional charge in these building blocks of Europeanism *in statu nascendi* is, of course, undeniable. The various kinds of totalitarian nationalist abuse, which in both nineteenth- and twentieth-century Europe have often afflicted the mobilizing power of collective emotional ties need not disqualify them from the equation. In fact, the dominant political currents in Europe's "age of extremes" offer copious evidence that primary national identifications based on the shared self-perception of the ethnic, cultural, and linguistic heritage have almost always won the competition for popular allegiance, leaving other kinds of identifications, based on social class or the lofty ideals of abstract cosmopolitanism, as second-place options.

Europeanism, then, is merely an "invented tradition" (as Eric Hobsbawn would say), which contains a fragile hope that its far-reaching, inclusive agenda might appeal to a majority of the citizens and peoples of Europe. So far, alas, precious few efforts have been made to construct such a common master narrative. In part, this is because Europe lacks a common natural language. Among the numerous national, ethnic, and cultural traditions on the continent, Europeanism does not figure very high on anyone's list of identities. Moreover, it would not be too excessive to claim that the systemic and institutional integration of the European continent increasingly diverges from cultural integration. It is with understandable regret that I must state the obvious: the European Union has not yet succeeded in building a satisfactory series of images, values, and ideals that would transcend our immediate existence with all its difficulties and joys. Europeanism—as an orderly constellation of aspirations, values, images, attitudes, convictions, and concepts that could serve as a source of individual inspiration and grant meaning to collective behavior—such Europeanism has not yet appeared on the horizon.

Nevertheless, I am convinced that it needs to be jointly contemplated and envisioned; otherwise, we all will find ourselves, rich West Europeans no less than poor Central and East Europeans, in an undesirable situation. We will share institutions and agencies overseeing free-flowing financial and labor transactions, but our respective cultural spheres will remain condemned to an existence of reciprocal tolerance at best, that is to say, mutually encouraged passivity and a lack of active interest in regard to each other's immediate experience, as Will Kymlicka suggests in *Multicultural Citizenship*. Without a broad social consensus on the legitimate and, thus, publicly recognized presence of a grand narrative in which Europeans can recognize themselves precisely as Europeans—and not exclusively as Poles, Germans, Lithuanians or Croatians—any attempt to construct such a narrative has to resort to abstract postulates. Therefore, it is hardly surprising that the development of a "common mental framework," in which the rich experience of European cultural diversity could be symbolically integrated and remodeled, faces greater difficulties in both form and substance than the development of a "common market." John Stuart Mill, in *Considerations on Representative Government,* expressed this need in a classic formulation: "Among a people without fellow feelings, especially if they read and speak different languages, the united public opinion necessary to the working of representative government cannot exist."

Supranational identifications presuppose the need to recognize multiple loyalties. Inasmuch as the diversity of cultures has traditionally been a key element of Europe's greatness, this very diversity should be reinforced and celebrated. The forging of a new European identity as a complex, hybrid invented tradition calls for the recognition of the ineluctably multiple identities from which Europeanism might be designed. There is, of course, an element of wishful thinking here: multilayered identities should allow for the simultaneous celebration of local, national, and continental elements. It should not be impossible to be at the same time Catalan, Spanish, and European. Basic allegiances need not be exclusivist allegiances.

Alas, the current strategies of the ongoing negotiation on the shape and character of Europeanism are to a large degree guided by a profound distrust of particular and national identifications. Such distrust may be understandable, but it is epistemologically unacceptable in a globalizing world in which Europeanism is itself but a particular identity. That is why it is impossible to fashion any common ground of shared European identity if one is forced to eschew fecund local and particular markers. If one shies away from the troublesome dialectics of particular and general, the only sustained answer will necessarily remain abstract and, ultimately, noncommittal. If one willfully avoids engaging the relevance of the cultural habits and values of the various nationalities of Europe, one's Europeanism will end up looking hollow, simulated, and insubstantial. Neither the authority of the European Commission nor the civic and ethnically blind character of Europe's supranational bodies possesses the ability to inspire citizens; these institutions are too hollow for any social mobilization and too immaterial to spark spontaneous affection, as John Keane has eloquently stated.

As I tried to calm down my excited children on the terrace of the Saint Francis Hotel in Assisi, I vaguely deliberated on this topic, as much as one can on a hot August afternoon. If my deliberations were disjointed and fragmented, a moment of truth was nonetheless approaching. As the dignified and reserved waiter brought the bill, Europeanism revealed itself in its full, miserable, and abstract nature. When I tried to pay with a bunch of new, hardly used euro banknotes, the waiter turned them down politely but firmly, just as he had undoubtedly learned to turn down suspicious-looking checks and bogus credit cards. More important than my annoyance at this inconvenience was the realization that there is, indeed, something artificial about euro banknotes. They are—if we look at them closely—completely lacking in character. To put it bluntly, they resemble a Europeanism imposed from above.

What visually distinguishes the five-euro bill is a picture of a vaguely ancient viaduct that could have been erected anywhere in the Roman Empire. The ten-euro bill boasts a Romanesque portal and bridge, while the two-hundred-euro bill, which I did not offer to the waiter, bears a less-than-clear image of a glass door and some kind of iron bridge. Unlike national currencies, the euro is too timid to show a face and too reticent to suggest a biography, to give pride of place to any story. Not a single human being appears on these crisp banknotes. Incapable of inspiring any sense of recognition, of *de te fabula narratur,* these notes are abstractions, ideas suggesting little, if any, tangible or familiar sensual quality. In vain one searches for portraits of such figures as Erasmus, Shakespeare, Michelangelo, Mickiewicz, Velasquez, Newton, Goethe, Andrić. The columns and arches on these notes suggest ruined empires, transformed into a nostalgia for connection and community, something lost in the sands of the irrecoverable past. This past is irrecoverable because it has no foundation, no recognizable landscape. The banknote imagery of the euro visually represents a no-man's land without historical memory. Currency can serve as a kind of collective ID card, which tells people they belong to a nation's imaginary community. What we must sadly infer from euro banknotes is that post-Maastricht Europe is a land with no founding event, destiny, or battle for independence— with, in fact, no real independence, if one considers America's increasingly reluctant security guarantees for the grand European experiment.

In this regard, Europe's weakest point, as I see it, is that it cannot offer enough transnational ideas that would function integratively and at the same time not rely solely on the laws of the free market. This failure concerns me not only in regard to the fragmentary cultural conditions of Europeanism; there are even more sinister effects. In the vacuum created by the lack of integrative works of the common imagination, many offshoots of political populism can flourish, since they are adept at using such simplistic and easy-to-understand metaphors as "a full boat" and "Fortress Europe," as Jean-Marie Le Pen has done in France and Jörg Haider in Austria, to mention but two notorious examples. These right-wing political metaphors have one goal in particular: to mask economic interests with ethnic slogans. These rhetorical appeals to an exclusiv-ist concern for one's own ethnic community seek to cover up the effects of globalization on the distribution of wealth and the erosion of the important European tradition of the social state. Since the political elite cannot deal criti-cally with transnational corporations, on which its survival increasingly de-pends, the simplest way to solve the problem is to make a scapegoat of foreign-ers, immigrants, and the Eastern masses (to say nothing of the third world). An enlightened segment of public still recognizes these outbursts of "fascism with a smile" as aberrant and unacceptable political behavior. The key issue, however, lies elsewhere. Expressions of chauvinistic populism, indeed, cannot be simply reduced to deviations from the norm but are, rather, a constituent part of an inte-gration process that concerns itself exclusively with the freedom of the market, which, in turn, ushers in the corporate homogenization of everyday life. The hidden handshake of solidarity once guaranteed by the social state and its safety nets has gone by the wayside.

In this context, one notices even more painfully that awareness of the need for a comprehensive, inclusive, and pluralistic grand narrative is articulated only in very vague terms. This vagueness, of course, is intimately linked to the willed, rational, and deliberate construction of such a grand European narrative. I have no illusions whatsoever about the "natural," "everlasting," or "stable" nature of founding narratives, which are always the provisional outcome of on-going negotiations over the choice of constitutive elements and their constella-tion. It is essential, however, that we agree on this: the construction of Europe-anism must be based on the entire field of cultural and ethnic traditions. The difficulties of reaching such a consensus present a series of practical impedi-ments to the project. Even more important than the undoubtedly large practical impediments is a poorly reflected basic presumption, which I have described as "metaphysical." It derives from the ambiguous use of the term "Europe"—and the corresponding public perception—which reserves the term for Western Europe or the European Union alone. The danger of such coterminous usage in political parlance was appallingly well revealed in the wars of Yugoslav succes-sion. The shameful role and calculated inactivity of the E.U. in the Balkan con-flict very bitterly exposed the fragile nature of the existing "European" grand narrative. For the longest time, the conflict was either dismissed as "tribal," "ethnic," and "primitive," or discussed solely in terms of humanitarian aid. It was not, by and large, viewed as a "European" conflict.

Euro-Skepticism and the Lessons of Yugoslavia

The Third Balkan War exploded the myth of a universal European idea, nascent though it may have been. As the misperceptions and consequent mismanage-ment of the admittedly difficult situation in the Balkans demonstrated, the feet of European unity are made of clay. It is their hollow idols, rather than their universal ideals, that Europeans worship according to their need and with regard

to the circumstances and the potential for profit. The victims of ethnic megalomania—in particular, the Bosnian Muslims, who revered and counted on the
European ideals of tolerance and peaceful coexistence, which proclaimed
"Never again!" to genocide—were made brutally aware of the essential relativ-
ity of "European" values.

The E.U.'s real priorities lie elsewhere, primarily in protecting the developed western part of Europe and deepening its integration, while concomitantly
guarding against the destabilizing effects of geopolitical changes in the eastern
part of the continent in general, and in the Balkans in particular. "Never again!"
as a guarantee against a repeat of catastrophe, seems—in its anguished migra-
tion over the past half-century—to have become limited to only to a certain part
of the continent, that is, to Western Europe proper. The mobilizing power of
moral consideration has thus been severely crippled. It has given way to a hap-
hazard strategy whose core organizing principle is to "throw money at the
problem."

From this vantage point, it is hardly surprising that in the post-communist
countries waiting to enter the club of the select, and in the E.U. member states
themselves, any form of doubt in the self-evident economic revelation and historical necessity of the E.U. is declared to be a dangerous step in the wrong direction. The "Euro-skeptical" attitude in public debates is, at the beginning of
the twenty-first century, hardly popular anywhere. How could it be? It must deal
with the unreflective but well-promoted assumption that any criticism of the
specific E.U. integration process comes from nationalistic, and thus, stuffy and
provincial, thinking. At the same time, Euro-skepticism is viewed, in fact, as an
unwelcome critique of the "European" way of thinking, with its rational debate
and emphasis on the common good.

The expanding web of ideas that feed on an unarticulated, often completely
emotional aversion to the European Union as the ultimate standard of public
behavior on the European continent is mind-boggling, though certainly not obvious. This conglomeration of counter-ideas and half-baked arguments does not
derive from a single source. Moreover, there are often contradictions between
these ideas. Yet with a certain degree of heuristic caution, one can identify four
main sources of Euro-skepticism. The first produces various kinds of aversion to
possible negative consequences of integration and the diminished significance of
state boundaries (the growth of organized crime, for example). The second is
inspired by a concern for protecting one's own ethnic identity (xenophobia),
while the third gains power from warnings about the E.U.'s nondemocratic ex-
ecutive bodies. The fourth source of Euro-skepticism stems from the failure to
form a "common mental framework."

The first two sources of Euro-skepticism are linked to the conservative anti-
European mindset. As such, they are of no interest for the present discussion.
The other two tendencies are closely connected. In my opinion, they are of
paramount importance and the future of Europe depends on their coordination.
These two concerns—let's call them progressive Euro-skeptical tendencies—
can be briefly described as follows: First, the application of the "European stan-

dard" is itself arbitrary. In other words, if the E.U., as a state entity, were to be scrutinized in the way aspirant countries are scrutinized in the process of integration, the E.U. itself would not qualify for membership because of its democratic deficit. The other form of Euro-skepticism, which is my main focus here, derives from the understanding that the E.U. is primarily an economic and security-oriented community. It has failed to develop "fellow feeling," common "habits of the heart" geared toward the common realization of common dreams. Europe, at the psychological level, requires elements that link the past as a support for collective memory with the future as the projection of common dreams, as Karl Cordell, among others, has forcefully argued in discussing the tensions between the European Union and nation-states.

A word of caution is needed, however. Europeanism as an attitude may help us in the effort to create egalitarian, democratic, and vibrant communities that render individual life secure and meaningful, but Europeanism as a requirement "from above," as *pro forma* cosmopolitanism, is more likely to rob us of concreteness and lived immediacy, unlocking something that ultimately may encourage less wholesome aspects of the yearning for the community and identity. If anything, Europe's experience in the twentieth century has made it possible for us, in hindsight, to acknowledge the enormous power of primary identifications. It makes no sense to dismiss them with liberal disdain. Our attachments, after all, start off parochially and only later expand outward. To bypass them in favor of an unmediated "European" identity is to risk ending up nowhere—to feel at home neither in our home nor in the world. Those who love humanity in general often cannot abide people in particular, as Moliere taught us in *The Misanthrope*. The prudent thing is to kindle an affection for the general by reveling in the particular. Allegiances to national or ethnic identities are not irrelevant, as many would have us believe. The question is, rather: How and on what grounds do we assess these allegiances, and, with respect to each, what kind of responsibility is involved in acknowledging them? It is imperative that we reflect on these choices. If the children of Europe are taught about the world "from part to whole," even as they are made familiar with the larger framework early on, they will have a basis from which to explore as much as they can about the world and, in turn, find ways to shift back and forth between concentric circles of identification, as Sissela Bok suggests in her essay "From Part to Whole."

In light of the difficulties that impede the construction of "Europeanism" as the outer rim of these concentric circles for European nations and individuals, one can do worse than point to the lesson of the former Yugoslavia. Yugoslavism was *mutatis mutandis* just such a "common framework." It was based on the Communist Party's ideological projection about the need to overcome particular national identifications and its promotion of a mythology of "brotherhood and unity." As such, Yugoslavism systematically tried to suppress ethnic particularities. It turned out, alas, that during this lengthy and richly orchestrated process "from above," the imposition of Yugoslavism also broke down the political structures of the country. In addition to the endemic corruption of Yugoslavia's "soft" communist system, as well as the cult of personality surrounding

Tito, its undisputed leader, the historical reasons for the collapse of this promising supranational identification have to be seen in tendencies toward autonomy
on the part of the constituent republics (which eventually gained the right to
conduct their own cultural affairs) and, above all, in a growing appetite for
domination by the largest national group, the Serbs, over the other, less numerous national groups, as Andrew Wachtel suggests in *Making a Nation, Breaking
a Nation: Literature and Cultural Politics in Yugoslavia* (1998).

The failure to create a synthetic Yugoslav culture that would not privilege
the tradition of the most numerous national group meant, to a large degree, that
the only strongholds available to increasingly manipulated ethnic aspirations
were those offered by the policies of the constituent republics. I believe we need
to refresh our suppressed memories of Yugoslavism as a potentially strong,
though abused, wax that could possibly have cemented disparate ethnic traditions. Nevertheless, this wax did manage to hold together the wings of a number
of South Slavic traditions for as long as they could agree on a common goal, that
is, until the early 1970s. But when this ambitious Icarus flew too high, the wax
quickly melted in the heat of nationalist self-sufficiency.

The European situation is, admittedly, more complex, since on the cultural
level one must deal with, on the one hand, resistance to Americanization and, on
the other, a competitive clash between the French and German versions of Europeanism. In the light of the Yugoslav lesson, however, attempts to force English
or German as the language of political life—and eventually, one assumes, as the
language of all other public spheres—cannot inspire high hopes for "Europeanism" as a genuinely shared and inclusive master narrative (even given the argument that a common language would be cheaper and easier for business).
Meanwhile, demands for consideration of cultural specificities, including the use
of language, carry an unpleasant ring. One need only recall the way Yugoslav
political rhetoric would accuse Slovenes or Macedonians of nationalism if, for
example, they wanted to exercise their constitutional right to speak in their
mother tongue in the Federal Yugoslav Parliament (where, officially, all the
constituent languages and nationalities were equal). This right, indeed, was
merely nominal and, for all practical purposes, proved illusory. If the nationalism of Europe's larger nations, both in the recent past and today, is something
normal, if it represents a general light in which all other lights are seen as particular ones, then it is no wonder that a Europeanism which takes its building
blocks from the cultural heritage of only the most populous and well-established
nations (Germany, France, England) fails to inspire me with any fervent hope
for a fairer, freer Europe.

A Feeble Common Mental Frame

From this perspective, the dangers of E.U. integration are particularly apparent
in the cultural sphere. As stated above, the E.U. was not created as a community
of values or shared memory, but as an economic structure. Economic pressure in

the service of unification uses the argument that any support for language differences or cultural specifics would lead to Balkanization and further nationalist conflict. Avoiding such division is often considered the first condition for establishing European identity.

The dilemma the E.U. faces is this: how to maintain the former inequality and at the same time demonstrate support for a program of equality? Let us recall that the E.U. is an organization chiefly designed for the benefit of large transnational corporations, which, of course, are bothered by political state borders. The global market was created not by the decisions of the majority in a democratic vote, but from a belief that large companies can grow faster without restrictions such as tariffs and taxes. In this regard, globalization provides a framework within which people attempt to remove obstacles to doing business. State boundaries, moral concepts, cultural traditions, specific daily rituals, frames of mind—that is, anything that impedes economic development is by definition seen as troublesome.

I know, of course, that cultural differences will not disappear overnight. I am not prophesying the dissolution of ethnic particularity or the consequent promotion of a European "melting pot"; I am aware that a more limited space does exist, and will continue to exist, for regional identities and local traditions. But I cannot rid myself of the feeling that the cultural diversity of Europe is acquiring folkloristic features (through tourism, heritage industries, etc.). If this is a strategy of survival among small European nations—particularly, the postcommunist countries—it is a bad political choice, since such a strategy is invariably defensive.

Given such diversity, we should be developing the conditions for intercultural competence, and not only a tolerance of difference. In contrast to the notion of tolerance—a highly evocative concept in the contemporary lexicon of "European" ideas—multicultural competence represents active curiosity and an effort to learn about less familiar cultures, an effort that will keep individuals and nations from locking themselves away within their own borders. Indeed, multicultural competence strengthens one's habits of self-reflection and self-evaluation. The concentric circles of multiple identities in the construction of Europeanism must derive from mutual respect, not from some hierarchical scale. The moment when a rhetoric of numbers and size takes over as the criterion for the participation of individual European nations in constructing a common mental framework, appreciation of cultural diversity is lost. Compared to other large geopolitical systems, Europe's cultural diversity is its greatest asset.

If we require individual nations to have a certain "critical mass" in order to make a valid contribution to the common master narrative, then we will soon find that we are living our lives along two increasingly divergent tracks. Public, bureaucratic, and economic life will be conducted in one of the two or three languages of the larger nations, while the private, domestic, and emotional life of individuals and ethnic groups will be conducted in the local languages of the smaller countries, languages condemned to dry up eventually or disappear altogether. Such bifurcation, indeed, encourages "museumization," folklorization, and the spread of cultural tourism. While these tendencies may appear in principle to represent a generosity of mind, they, in fact, foster conditions for insular and egotistical cultural voyeurism, which has little to do with the multicultural competence Europe needs.

Because of an easier, more efficient integration adhering to the exclusive standards of "economism" instead of an inclusive Europeanism, there is a good possibility that the smaller pastoral, exotic, rural languages will, paradoxically, confirm Marx's arrogant definition of "non-historical nations." I am, of course, fully aware that it will be extremely expensive to maintain the diversity of Europe's cultures, languages, and ethnic traditions. But I also know that this is vital if we are to construct a common narrative of mutual allegiance, one in which the nations of Europe can fulfill the hope expressed by the Slovene Romantic poet, France Prešeren: "That all men free / No more shall foes, but neighbors be."

References

Adamic, Louis. *Struggle*. Los Angeles: A. Whipple, 1934.

————. *The Native's Return: An American Immigrant Visits Yugoslavia and Discovers His Old Country*. New York: Harper & Brothers, 1934.

Ady, Endre. *Új Versek* [New Poems]. Budapest: Eötvös, 1989. First published in 1906.

Andrić, Ivo. *The Bridge on the Drina*. New York: Macmillan, 1959.

Arns, Inke. *Neue Slowenische Kunst. NSK. Eine Analyse ihrer künstlerischen Strategien im Kontext der 1980er Jahre in Jugoslawien*. Regensburg: Museum Ostdeutsche Galerie, 2002.

Ash, Timothy Garton. *History of the Present: Essays, Sketches and Dispatches from Europe in the 1990s*. London: Allen Lane, 1999.

Barber, Benjamin. *Jihad vs. McWorld: How Globalism and Tribalism Are Reshaping the World*. New York: Ballantine Books, 1995.

Bauman, Zygmunt. *Life in Fragments: Essays in Postmodern Morality*. New York: Blackwell, 1995.

————. *Liquid Modernity*. New York: Blackwell, 2000.

Bellah, Robert, et al. *Habits of the Heart: Individualism and Commitment in American Life*. New York: Harper & Row, 1985.

Benjamin, Walter. *One-Way Street, and Other Writings*. London: NLB, 1979.

Berman, Russel A. *Modern Culture and Critical Theory: Art, Politics, and the Legacy of the Frankfurt School*. Madison: University of Wisconsin Press, 1989.

Blatnik, Andrej. *Skinswaps*. Evanston, Ill.: Northwestern University Press, 1998.

Bloom, Harold. *The Anxiety of Influence: A Theory of Poetry*. London: Oxford University Press, 1975.

Bok, Sissela. "From Part to Whole." In *For Love of the Country: Debating the Limits of Patriotism*, edited by J. Cohen. Boston: Beacon Press, 1996.

Brodsky, Joseph. "To Please a Shadow." In *Less Than One: Selected Essays*. New York: Farrar, Straus & Giroux, 1986. First published in 1983.

Cankar, Ivan. *Zbrano delo* [Collected works]. Vol. 9, *Tujci; Ob zori; Nezbrane črtice*

1900–1902 [Strangers; At daybreak; Uncollected sketches 1900–1902]. Ljubljana: Državna založba Slovenije, 1970.

———. *Zbrano delo* [Collected Works]. Vol. 18, *Sosed Luka; Kurent; Črtice in novele (1907–1909)* [Neighbor Luka; Kurent; Sketches and novellas 1907–1909]. Ljubljana: Državna založba Slovenije, 1973.

Cordell, Karl. "European Union and Nation-State: The Politics of Hope Encounters the Politics of Experience." *The European Legacy* 1, no. 2 (1996): 710–719.

Davis, Robert Murray. "Slovene Writing After Independence." *World Literature Today* 75 (2001): 59–69.

Debeljak, Aleš. *Anxious Moments*. Fredonia, N.Y.: White Pine Press, 1994.

———. "A Haven of Free Speech: The Story of *Nova revija* in Slovenia." *Budapest Review of Books* 6, no. 3 (fall 1996): 149–152.

———. *Postmoderna sfinga: kontinuteta modernosti in postmodernosti* [Postmodern sphinx: The continuity of modernity and postmodernity]. Ljubljana: Wieser, 1989.

———. *Reluctant Modernity: The Institution of Art and its Historical Forms*. Lanham, Md.: Rowman & Littlefield, 1998.

———. "Slovenia: A Brief Literary History." In *Afterwards: Slovenian Writing, 1945–1995*, edited by Andrew Zawacki. Buffalo, N.Y.: White Pine Press, 1999.

———. *Twilight of the Idols: Recollections of a Lost Yugoslavia*. Fredonia, N.Y.: White Pine Press, 1994.

Debeljak, Aleš, ed. *The Imagination of Terra Incognita: Slovenian Writing, 1954–1995*. Fredonia, N.Y.: White Pine Press, 1997.

———. *Prisoners of Freedom: Contemporary Slovenian Poetry*. Santa Fe, N.M.: Pedernal Press, 1993.

Flisar, Evald. *My Father's Dreams: A Tale of Innocence Abused*. Norman, Okla.: Texture Press, 2002.

Friedrich, Hugo. *Die Struktur der modernen Lyrik: von Baudelaire bis zur Gegenwart* [The structure of the modern lyric]. Hamburg: Rowohlts, 1956.

Grafenauer, Niko. *Palimpsesti*. Ljubljana: Mladinska knjiga, 1984.

Hart, Kevin. "Review of Tomaž Šalamun's *Feast* and *Ballad for Metka Krašovec*." *Verse* 18 (2001): 209–213.

Hass, Robert. *Twentieth Century Pleasures: Prose on Poetry*. New York: Ecco Press, 1984.

Huyssen, Andreas. *Twilight Memories: Marking Time in a Culture of Amnesia*. New York: Routledge, 1995.

Jackson, Richard, ed. *Double Vision: Four Slovenian Poets: Aleš Debeljak, Alojz Ihan, Brane Mozetič, Jure Potokar*. Ljubljana: Aleph; Chattanooga, Tenn.: Poetry Miscellany Books, 1993.

Jameson, Frederic. *Postmodernism, or, The Cultural Logic of Late Capitalism*. Durham, N.C.: Duke University Press, 1984.

Jančar, Drago. *Mocking Desire*. Translated by Michael Biggins. Evanston, Ill.: Northwestern University Press, 1998.

———. *Northern Lights*. Translated by Michael Biggins. Evanston, Ill.: Northwestern University Press, 2001.

Jančar, Drago, et al. *The Day Tito Died: Contemporary Slovenian Short Stories*. London: Forest Books, 1993.

Jarc, Miran. *Človek in noč* [Man and the night]. Ljubljana: published by the author, 1927.

Karahasan, Dževad. *Sarajevo, Exodus of a City*. New York: Kodansha, 1994.

Keane, John. "Nations, Nationalism and European Citizens." In *Notions of Nationalism,* edited by Sukumar Periwal. Budapest: Central European University Press, 1995.

Keats, John. *Letters of John Keats.* Selected by Frederick Page. The World's Classics, no. 541. London: Oxford University Press, 1954.

Kideckel, David. "Us and Them: Concepts of East and West in the East European Tradition." In *Cultural Dilemmas of Post-Communist Societies,* edited by A. Jawowska and M. Kempny. Warsaw: IFIS Publications, 1994.

Kiš, Danilo. *Homo Poeticus. Essays and Interviews.* New York: Farrar, Straus and Giroux, 1995.

————. *A Tomb for Boris Davidovich.* New York: Harcourt Brace Jovanovich, 1978.

Kocbek, Edvard. *Embers in the House of Night: Selected Poems.* Translated by Sonja Kravanja. Santa Fe, N.M.: Lumen, 1999.

Kosovel, Srečko. "Razpad družbe in propad umetnosti" [The disintegration of society and the decline of art, 1925]. *Zbrana dela* [Collected works] 3. Ljubljana: DZS, 1977.

Kosztolányi, Dezso. *Darker Muses.* Budapest: Corvina, 1990.

Krečič, Peter. *Plečnik: The Complete Works.* New York: Whitney Library of Design, 1993.

Kreft, Lev. "Ljubljana." In *Central European Avant-Gardes: Exchange and Transformation, 1910–1930,* edited by Timothy O. Benson. Cambridge: MIT Press, 2002. Pp. 284–287.

Kundera, Milan. "The Tragedy of Central Europe." *New York Review of Books* 31, no. 7 (1984): 33–38.

Kymlicka, Will. *Multicultural Citizenship: A Liberal Theory of Minority Rights.* Oxford: Clarendon Press, 1995.

Linhart, Anton Tomaž. *Miss Jenny Love.* Ljubljana: Slovensko narodno gledališče, 1967.

Lukács, John. *Budapest 1900: A Historical Portrait of the City and its Culture.* London: Weidenfeld & Nicolson, 1988.

Mannheim, Karl. *Ideology and Utopia: An Introduction to the Sociology of Knowledge.* San Diego: Harcourt Brace Jovanovich, 1985. Originally published in 1929.

Mastnak, Tomaž. *Crusading Peace: Christendom, the Muslim World, and Western Political Order.* Berkeley: University of California Press, 2001.

McClure, Robert. "Intelligent Patriotism." *Maxwell Perspective* 12, no. 2 (2002).

Melucci, Alberto. "Co-existing with Differences." *2B: Journal of Ideas,* no. 13 (1998): 140–141.

Merrill, Christopher. *Only the Nails Remain: Scenes from the Balkan Wars.* Lanham, Md.: Rowman & Littlefield, 1999.

Mikeln, Miloš. *Veliki voz.* Ljubljana: Mihelač, 1992.

Mill, John Stuart. *Considerations on Representative Government.* New York: Forum Books, 1958.

Moisi, Dominique. "Dreaming of Europe." *Foreign Affairs,* no. 115 (summer 1999): 44–61.

Montenegro, David. *Points of Departure: International Writers on Writing and Politics.* Ann Arbor: University of Michigan Press, 1991.

Morrison, Toni. *Song of Solomon.* New York: Alfred A. Knopf, 1977.

Morton, Frederic. *Nervous Splendor: Vienna 1888–89.* London: Weidenfeld & Nicolson, 1980.

Novak, Boris A. *Mojster nespečnosti* [The master of insomnia]. Ljubljana: Mladinska knjiga, 1995.

Orwell, George. "Politics and the English Language." In *Collected Essays.* London: Secker & Warburg, 1961. First published in 1946.

Pahor, Boris. *Edvard Kocbek: Pričevalec našega časa* [Edvard Kocbek: A witness of our time]. Trieste: Zaliv, 1975.
———. *Pilgrim Among the Shadows*. New York: Harcourt Brace, 1995.
Pirjevec, Dušan. *Vprašanje o poeziji, vprašanje naroda* [The question of poetry, the question of nation]. Maribor: Obzorja, 1978.
Plut-Pregelj, Leopoldina, and Carole Rogel. *Historical Dictionary of Slovenia*. London: Scarecrow Press, 1996.
Popa, Vasko. *Earth Erect*. Iowa City: University of Iowa Press, 1973.
Potokar, Ludve. *Krivi vir* [The guilty source]. In *Onstran samote* [On the other side of loneliness], edited by France Pibernik. Celje: Mohorjeva zalozba, 1995.
Prešeren, France. *Poems*. Kranj: Hermagoras, 2001.
Rizman, Rudi. "The Relevance of Nationalism for Democratic Citizenship." *The Public* 7, no. 1 (April 2000): 5–13.
Rožanc, Marjan. *Ljubezen* [Love]. Ljubljana: Mladinska knjiga, 1979.
———. "The Neoplatonic Cosmos." Translated by Erica Johnson-Debeljak. In *The Imagination of Terra Incognita: Slovenian Writing, 1954–1995*, edited by Aleš Debeljak. Fredonia: White Pine Press, 1997.
Rushdie, Salman. *Imaginary Homelands: Essays and Criticism, 1981–1991*. London: Granta Books, 1991.
Šalamun, Tomaž. *The Four Questions of Melancholy: New and Selected Poems*, edited by Christopher Merrill. Fredonia, N.Y.: White Pine Press, 1997.
———. *Poker*. Ljubljana: published by author, 1966.
———. *Praznik* [Celebration]. Ljubljana: Cankarjeva založba, 1976.
———. *The Selected Poems of Tomaž Šalamun*. New York: Ecco Press, 1988.
Sassower, Raphael and Louis Cicotello. *The Golden Avant-Garde: Idolatry, Commercialism, and Art*. Charlottesville: University Press of Virginia, 2000.
Schumer, Dirk. "Modern Slavery." *Frankfurter Allgemeine Zeitung* (English edition), March 28, 2001.
Shell, Marc, and Werner Sollors, eds. *The Multilingual Anthology of American Literature: A Reader of Original Texts with English Translations*. New York: New York University Press, 2000.
Svit, Brina. *Con Brio*. London: Harvill Press, 2002.
Tamir, Yael. *Liberal Nationalism*. Princetown: Princeton University Press, 1993.
Vidmar, Josip. *Kulturni problem slovenstva* [The cultural problem of Slovene identity]. Ljubljana: Cankarjeva založba, 1995. First published in 1932.
Wachtel, Andrew. *Making a Nation, Breaking a Nation: Literature and Cultural Politics in Yugoslavia*. Stanford: Stanford University Press, 1998.
Wells, Herbert G. *The Time Machine*. London: Longman, 1971. First published in 1895.
Zagajewski, Adam. *Tremor: Selected Poems*. New York: Farrar, Strauss and Giroux, 1985.
Zajc, Dane. *Barren Harvest*. Buffalo, N.Y.: White Pine Press, 2004.

Index

Ady, Endre, 89
aesthetic, 77
aesthetic dogma, 71–72
aestheticism, 72–75; commodity of, 77;
  contemporary, 70; formalist, 66;
  latter-day, 66; politics of, 65–67;
  truth of, 80; vision of, 78
aesthetization, of the everyday world,
  76–93
Ambergris (Šalamun), 68
America: arts and culture of, 37, 52–56;
  the condition of, 26; Europe and, 54;
  national tradition of, 27; self-reliance
  in, 26; Slovene absence in, 50;
  Slovene literature in, 48; Slovene
  response to, 48; social, intellectual,
  and cultural advantages of, 53;
  values of, 26. *See also* literature;
  poetry
America (Šalamun), 39
Anderson, Benedict, 32, 83
Andrič, Ivo, 38
The Anxiety of Influence (Bloom), 33
archetype, city as an, 79–82
art: aesthetic layer of, 74–78; American
  pop, 75; autonomy of, 65, 70–71, 83;
  city's influence on, 81; collective life
  and, 62; communism and, 63–65, 72;

contemporary, 75; European, 83;
  excellence in, 66; historical
  framework for, 71; immortality of,
  40–42; individual and, 77; language
  and, 67; life and, 67, 70; national
  community and, 79, 83; national
  identity and, 82; politics and, 90;
  post–World War II, 74; Slovenia
  and, 83; social consequences of, 79;
  vision and testimony of, 67–71. *See
  also* avant-garde; modernism;
  Slovenia
artists: civic identity and, 15;
  expatriate, twentieth-century, 35;
  isolation of, 37. *See also* avant-garde
Ash, Timothy Garton, 100
Ashbery, John, 36, 54
Austria, 20. *See also* Vienna
Austro-Hungarian Empire: collapse of,
  59, 67; Yugoslavia and, 12
avant-garde: artists of, 72; historical,
  76–77; Slovenia and, 71–74, 76

Balkan Wars, 21, 38, 105
Balkans, 4, 68; cultural traditions of,
  17; European Union and, 105
Barbaropa (Ehrenstein), 67
Barber, Benjamin, 22–23

Index

Barthes, Roland, 43, 72
Baudrillard, Jean, 1, 56
Bauhaus, 87
Bauman, Zygmunt, 5, 23
Bazlen, Roberto "Bob," 60, 87
Belgium, 20
Bellah, Robert, 29
Benjamin, Walter, 63, 69, 80
Berlin Wall, 98
Berman, Russell, 77
The Big Dipper (Mikeln), 33
bilingualism, 84–86
Blatnik, Andrej, 41
Bloom, Harold, 33
Bok, Sissela, 107
Bosnia, 23
The Bridge on the Drina (Andrič), 38
Brodsky, Joseph, 11, 81, 85
Budapest, 87–89
Budapest 1900 (Lukács), 84

Cankar, Ivan, 42, 65, 79-86
capitalism, xi, 77
Célan, Paul, 33, 66
*Central European Avant-Gardes:
   Exchanges and Transformation*
   (Kreft), 76
Churchill, Winston, 98
Cicotello, Louis, 75
citizenship: global, ix; identity and, 22;
   notion of, xiii
civic identity: benefits of, 15–16;
   cosmopolitanism and, 18; nation size
   and, 16. *See also* artists; patriotism
"Coexisting with Differences"
   (Melucci), 18
Cold War, 59; European effects of, x,
   96, 100; political and cultural
   institutions of, 96
collective: behavior of, 103; ethnic, 44;
   narrative of, 8–10, 94; tradition of, 8,
   32, 42, 45
collective experience, 19; literature
   and, 43, 74; Slovene, 46; subjective
   and, 79
collective history, 65
collective identity, 7, 31; assimilation
   through, 29; commitment to, 31;
   currency of, 104; national and global
   aspects of, 19

collective life, 2; art and, 62; Slovene,
   90
collective memory, 61–62, 64, 107
collective mentality, 6–8; literature and,
   34
collective solidarity, hidden handshake
   of, 23
common customs, 31
common mental frame, 108–10
common narrative, 110
communism, 2; art and, 63–65, 72;
   deterioration of, 95; legacy of, 94;
   manipulation by, 63; national
   identity and, 107; Neue Slowenische
   Kunst (NSK), 76; political and social
   heritage of, 40; post, 63, 84;
   recognizable frame of reference of,
   41; restrictions of, 39
community, 3–4; dialectic of, ix;
   ethnic, 105; multicultural and
   multireligious, 5; territory defining, x
*Considerations on Representative
   Government* (Mill), 103
Contemporary Slovenian Short Stories,
   40
corporations, 2, 109
cosmopolitanism, 18, 59–92, 102;
   competence of, 84; enhancement of,
   18; Europeanism, 107;
   parochialism's attack on, 18;
   Slovene writers and, 91; urban
   sensibilities and, 89. *See also* civic
   identity
"Crngrob" (Grafenauer), 33
cross-cultural pollination, 15
*Crusading Peace: Christendom, the
   Muslim World, and Western Political
   Order* (Mastnak), 96
"Cultural Capital of Europe," 101
cultural context: recognizing, 39–40;
   Slovenia's place within international,
   42
cultural heritage: individual literary
   expression and, 33; national, 7;
   paralysis of, 27–28; pride of, 8;
   stories and, 29
cultural identity: dual, 16–18; language
   and, 10; Slovene, 9, 14
cultural-linguistic tradition. *See*
   Germany

cultural memory, 7; totality of, 65
The Cultural Problems of Slovenian Identity (Vidmar), 17
cultural tourism, 110
culture, 5; collective life preserved by, 2; dominant, 12; global, x; national, 12, 23

Danish People's Party, 20
Darker Muses (Kosztolányi), 86
Davis, Robert Murray, 78
The Day Tito Died, 40
Debeljak, Aleš, works of, 47, 49, 56, 63, 64, 72, 76
democratic order, 22; institutions and, x; social, 70. *See also* nation-state
Denmark, 20
dialectic, ix
"The Disintegration of Society and the Decline of Art" (Kosovel), 21
"Doing and Undoing" (Novak), 70
"A Dreamer's Farewell to the New Country: Memories of Slovenia" (Handke), 47
"Dreaming of Europe" (Moisi), 102
Dreiser, Theodore, 44
Duino Elegies (Rilke), 60
"Duma" (Šalamun), 31–32
"Duma" (Žunpančič), 32

Earth Feet (Popa), 38
Eastern Europe, 94–98
economism, 101
ECSC (European Coal and Steel Community), 99
Ehrenstein, Albert, 67
Eliot, T. S., 66, 73
empires, multinational, 1
Enlightenment, the, 5, 19, 70, 85, 96
ethnic, 108. *See also* collective; community; exclusivism; immigration; tradition
ethnically based state, 5
ethnic fundamentalism, 21
ethnic identity, 5, 22; allegiance to, 107; mixing of, 20; nation size and, 16; protection of, 106; Slovene, 14
E.U. *See* European Union (E.U.)
euro banknotes, 104
Europe, 96–100; America and, 54; art of, 83; changing map of, 97; common mental framework within, 103, 106; cosmopolitan, 84; cultural and, 88, 102–3, 109; exclusivism of, 96; Hungary and, 88; identity of, 96–97, 101–5, 107–9; integration of, 98, 100, 105; literary patriarch of, 86; literature of, 80; nationalism of, 108; "paradise lost" of, 39; post-communist, 73; post-Maastricht, 104; post–World War I, 67; Slovenes in cultural current of, 86; social conditions of, 21; values of, 106; World War II and, 59, 96, 97. *See also* Eastern Europe; Europeanism; Western Europe
European Coal and Steel Community (ECSC), 99
European Commission, 4, 103
Europeanism, 97, 102–4; cosmopolitanism and, 107; cultural and ethnic traditions in, 105; French and German, 108; identity and, 102–3, 109; inclusive, 110; reconstruction of, 98–105
European Union (E.U.): administrative seat of, 16; candidate nations of, 4; common currency in, 21; economy of, 101, 107, 108; expansion of, 96; high standard of living in, 20; hybridity of, xii; immigration to, 19–21; individuality within, 12; integration process of, 19, 106, 108; Maastricht Treaty and, 95; Magyar people within, 20; member states of, 106; myth of, 100; Slovenia and, 4; unification of, 97–99. *See also* Balkans; Eastern Europe; nation-state; Western Europe
Euro-skepticism, 106
exclusivism, 22
excommunitari, 19
existentialism, 74

Fascists, 60, 64
Flemish Bloc, 20
foreigners, and natives, 13–14
The Four Questions of Melancholy (Šalamun), 68
France, 20

Freedom Party, 20
Free Territory of Trieste, 59
French Revolution, 5
Friedrich, Hugo, 72
Fromm, Erich, 9
"From Part to Whole" (Bok), 107
Fukuyama, Francis, 1, 74

Gaj, Ljudevit, 17
genocide, 4
Germany, 10, 13; cultural influence of,
84; cultural-linguistic, tradition, 13;
government program of, 21;
Romanticism, 5; unification of, 21
global integration, 13
globalization, 1–24, 103, 105, 109
global markets, 2
"global village," 7, 26, 40
The Golden Avant-Garde (Cicotello,
Sassower), 75
Grafenauer, Niko, 33
Great Britain, 20
The Guilty Source (Potokar), 44

Habits of the Heart (Bellah), 29
Haider, Jörg, 20, 104
Handke, Peter, 47, 90
Harlem Renaissance, 30
Hart, Kevin, 39
"A Haven of Free Speech: The Story of
Nova Revija in Slovenia" (Debeljak),
63
Heaney, Seamus, 45–46
historical consciousness, 61
Historical Dictionary of Slovenia, 43
history, 63–65; cultural and social, 6–7;
psychology and philosophy of, 61.
See also collective, narrative of
History of the Present (Ash), 100
Hitler, Adolf. *See* Home Guard
home: archetype symbol of, 80; city as,
81; existential need for, 28–31;
search for, 57
Home Guard: oath to Hitler by, 64;
Partisan resistance war with, 33
homogenization, 22, 105
House of Freedoms, 20
Hungary: artists of, 84, 89; culture of,
84; foreign policy of, 19; German
cultural influence on, 84; Slovenia

and, 84, 85, 87. *See also* Europe;
national identity
Huyssen, Andreas, 61

identity: context for, 94; framework of,
28; integral, 26; isolation and, 36–
39; separation of ethnic and civic,
16–18. *See also* civic identity;
collective identity; cultural identity;
ethnic identity; Europeanism;
individual; national identity
Ideology and Utopia (Mannheim), 73–
74
Illyrian tradition, 16–17
immigration, 18–21; ethnic
endangerment of, 21; political parties
against, 20
Imperial and Royal House of Habsburg,
85, 88
individual: endeavor of, 27; experience,
27; identity of, 12, 102; transcending
of, 28
*Individualism and Literary Metaphors
of Nationality,* xii
internationalism, ix, 18
Iron Curtain, 88, 97
Italy, 20, 60
"The Ivory tower" (Novak), 69

Jameson, Frederic, 52
Jančar, Drago, 48, 89–91
Jarc, Milan, 7
Jihad vs. McWorld (Barber), 22–23
Joyce, James, 15, 36, 60
Juričič, Josip, 62

Karahasan, Dževad, 78, 81
Keane, John, 22–23, 31, 104
Keats, John, 66
Kidecke, David, 97
Kiš, Danilo, 38, 54, 79
Kocbek, Edvard, 9, 48, 64, 65
Kosovel, Srečko, 21, 48, 65
Kosztolányi, Dezso, 86
Krečič, Peter, 83
Kovačič, Lojze, 33
Kreft, Lev, 76
Kristeva, Julia, 56
Kundera, Milan, 40–42, 81
"Kurent" (Cankar), 81, 82

Kymlicka, Will, 103

language, 10–13; artistic, 67;
bilingualism, 84–86; common, 31;
cultural experience and, 23; literature
and, 43–45, 54; mother tongue,
boundaries of, 57, 89; mother
tongue, confidence manifested in,
31; mother tongue, national
experience and, 11; mother tongue,
primacy of, 50; mother tongue,
writing in, 84; national, 1, 10, 34–36,
90; native, 14, 35; poetry and, 51;
Slovene, 10–12, 14, 17; Slovene
literature and, 39–40, 43, 51–52;
trans-rational, 37
L=A=N=G=U=A=G=E. *See* poetry
League of Nations, 21
Levstik, Fran, 13
Liberal Nationalism (Tamir), xiii
Life in Fragments (Bauman), 23
"The Lippizaners" (Kocbek), 9
Liquid Modernity (Bauman), 5
Literatura, 71, 73
literature: American, 53–54; Central
and Eastern European, 84; collective
experience and, 43, 74; collective
mentality and, 34; cultural
framework of, 33; international
styles of, 44; language and, 90;
national cultural identity and, 44;
politics and, 65; post-communist, 79;
Slovene, 33, 44, 72, 73, 78–84;
traditional, 51; transcending aspects
of, 67; truth of, 30. *See also*
modernism; mythology
Lithuania, 19
Ljubljana, 3, 87
Love (Rožanc), 3
lyric image, 68

Maastricht Treaty, 95. *See* European
Union (E.U.)
Making a Nation, Breaking a Nation
(Wachtel), 17, 108
Mallarme, Stephane, 74
Malucci, Alberto, 18
Man and the Night (Jarc), 7
Mannheim, Karl, 73–74, 84
Marshall Plan, 97

The Master of Insomnia (Novak), 69–
71
Mastnak, Tomaž, 96
"Melancholie des Abends" (Trakl), 80
memory. *See* collective memory;
cultural memory
Merrill, Christopher, 46, 49
Mikeln, Miloš, 33
Mill, John Stuart, 103
Milosz, Czeslaw, 36, 66, 94
Mocking Desire (Jančar), 48
Modern Culture and Critical Theory
(Berman), 77
modernism, 66, 74–77
"Modern Slavery" (Schumer), 19
Moisi, Dominique, 102
Monnet, Jean, 99
Morrison, Toni, 28–31
Multicultural Citizenship (Kymlicka),
103
*The Multilingual Anthology of
American Literature: A Reader of
Original Texts with English
Translations* (Shell, Sollors), 44
Murn, Josip, 37, 47
Muslims, 96
"My First Time in New York City"
(Šalamun), 57
mythology, 52–55, 80, 82; American,
25–26, 48; art and literature, 52;
European ideal, 105; history and, 75;
national, 8; national identity and, 31–
34; secular, 26, 31–34; Serbian, 38,
50; Slovene, 8–9, 32, 47

Nabokov, Vladimir, 85
national collective, 70, 82
national community, art and, 79, 83
national culture: experience of, 57;
inspiration of, 40–42
National Front, 20
national identity, 23, 27, 45, 102–3;
communism and, 107; Hungarian,
88; literature and, 44, 89; mythology
and, 31–34; preserving cultural
uniqueness of, 88; scope and purpose
of, 70–71. *See also* language;
Slovenia
nationalism, ix, x, 4, 5–6, 11, 72;
European, 108; size of country and,

98

nationalist conservatives, 18

nationality, 57

national stereotypes, 59–62

national traditions: attitude toward, 21–23; national language and, 34–36; parochial limitations of, ix; preservation of, 12; Slovene, writing from, 36

"Nations, Nationalism and European Citizens" (Keane), 22–23, 31

nation-state, 1–2, 4; art's place within, 62; democratic, 16, 22–23; ethnic unity in, 5; European Union, 107; globalization and, 4; public life as regulated by, 23; size of, 17; Slovene, 2, 9; territory of, x. *See also* civic identity; ethnic identity

native language, 14, 35

"native realm," 7

The Native's Return (Adamic), 44

Nazis, 64

"The Neoplatonic Cosmos" (Rožanc), 56

Netherlands, 20

Neue Slowenische Kunst (NSK), 76

The New York Review of Books, 40

Northern Lights (Jančar), 90–91

Novak, Boris A., and Šalamun, Tomaž, 67–71

NSK (Neue Slowenische Kunst), 76

OEEC (Organization for European Economic Corporation), 97

Old World, 25

"One-Way Street" (Benjamin), 80

Only the Nails Remain: Scenes from the Balkan War (Merrill), 46

Organization for European Economic Corporation (OEEC), 97

Orwell, George, 5

Pahor, Borís, 60, 64

Partisan resistance, 33

Pascal, Blaise, 99–100

patriotism, 4–6; civic identity and, 16; constitutional, 5, 16

People's Party, 20

Perelman, Bob, 51

personal identity, 80

personal vision, 28–31

Pirjevec, Dušan, 72, 74

Plečnik, Jože, xi, 42, 83

Plečnik: The Complete Works (Krečič), 83

poetry: American L=A=N=G=U=A=G=E school of, 51; books of, 40, 56, 72, 79, 89; collective context for, 52 contemporary Irish, 45–46; lyric, 78; native language and, 35; postmodernism and, 52; revealing nature of, 69–71; Slovene, 54–58, 85. *See also* Prešeren, France

Poker (Šalamun), 37

Poland: anticommunist patriotic forces in, 64; borders of, 19; Roman Catholic Church in, 64

political economy of insecurity, 93–94

"Politics and the English Language" (Orwell), 5

Popa, Vasko, 38, 81

Postmodernism, or, The Cultural Logic of Late Capitalism (Jameson), 52

Postmodern Sphinx (Debeljak), 76

Potokar, Ludve, 44

Prešeren, France, 7, 10, 46, 65, 110

radical individualism, 26–27, 39

reism, 51

"The Relevance of Nationalism for Democratic Citizenship" (Rizman), 1

responsible citizenship, 100

Reynolds, J. H., 66

Rilke, Rainer Maria, 15, 60

Rizman, Rudi, 1

Roman Catholic Church, in Poland, 64

Rožanc, Marjan, 3, 56–57

Rushdie, Salman, 32–34

Šalamun, Tomaž, 31–32, 37, 45–51, 55, 57, 89; aesthetic impulses of, 67; exploration of formal structure by, 67; Novak, Boris A. and, 67–71; personal tradition of, 50

Sarajevo, Exodus of a City (Karajasan), 78

Sassower, Raphael, 75

Schengen Treaty, 19

Schumer, Dirk, 19

Schumman, Robert, 99
Schurtz, Karl, 6
The Selected Poems of Tomaž Šalamun,
37, 45
self: autonomous, 26; dialectic of, ix
Serbia: Balkans and, 13; dominance of,
38; military of, 13, 38; mythology,
38, 50; politics of, 13
Shell, Marc, 44
Simic, Charles, 37, 50
Skinswaps (Blatnik), 41
"Slovene Writing After Independence"
(Davis), 78
Slovenia, ix; artists of, 42; avant-garde
art in, 51, 73; avant-garde
movements of, 51; constructivism in,
87; culture of, 9, 13–14, 42–45, 47,
50, 71, 86; dualism of, 49, 79;
émigré writers of, 44; ethnicity
within, 14, 59, 64; European Union
and, 4; foreigners and, 13–15, 46;
freedoms in, 73; German cultural
influence on, 84; Hungary, 84, 85,
87; isolation of, 36, 39, 94; literary
modernism of, 37, 79, 82–84; literary
movement of, reism, 51; literature of,
33–34, 39–40, 42–45, 57, 62, 79;
lyrical tradition of, 54, 56;
mythology of, 8–9, 32, 47; national
identity of, 32, 45; national
sovereignty of, 2–3, 4, 9, 62; Nazi-
occupied, 33; parochialism of, 83;
political context for, 13; Socialist
Republic of, 13, 59; traditions of, xii,
50; transitional society of, 79;
Trieste's importance to, 59–60; wars
of, x, 33, 46, 64; World War I and,
65; World War II and, 3, 33; writing
of, 78; Yugoslavia and, 2, 13, 38, 89.
See also America; collective
experience; collective life;
cosmopolitanism; Home Guard;
language; poetry
"Slovenia: A Brief Literary History"
(Debeljak), 47
social class, ix, 2
social Darwinism, 26
social democracy, 25
Socialist Federation. *See* Slovenia
socialization: Irish primary, 45–46;

primary, 7
society, 25
solidarity, moral and political, 4
Sollors, Werner, 44
Song of Solomon (Morrison), 28–31
Sontag, Susan, 28
Soviet Bloc countries, 84
Soviet Union, former, 21
Spain, 20
Strangers (Cankar), 83
Strniša, Gregor, 51, 74
structure, monarchial, 1
The Structure of the Modern Lyric
(Friedrich), 72
Struggle (Adamic), 44
Supreme Ideal, 5–6

The Time Machine (Wells), 23
Tito's Partisans, 33, 64, 108
"To Please a Shadow" (Brodsky), 11
A Tomb for Boris Davidovich (Kiš), 38
Tomšič, Marjan, 33, 60
Totenfuge? (Célan), 66
tradition: American national, 27;
balance between ethnic and cultural,
102; cultural, and individual talent,
90; ethnic, 5, 12, 102, 108; fading of
single, xii; liberation of self from,
82; Slovene creative, 57. *See also*
collective; national collective
"The Tragedy of Central Europe"
(Kundera), 40
Trakl, Georg, 67, 80
transnational ideas, 104
Treaty of Rome, 95
Treaty of Trianon, 19
Tremor (Zagajewski), 36
Trotsky, Leon, 86
truth, 5–6
Twilight Memories (Huyssen), 61
*Twilight of the Idols: Recollections of a
Lost Yugoslavia* (Debeljak), 64

Ukraine, 19
United Nations, 59
"Us and Them: Concepts of East and
West in the Eastern European
Transition" (Kidecke), 97

Velvet Revolutions, 19, 40, 74, 98

"Versailles" (Šalamun), 68–69
Verse (Hart), 39
Vidmar, Josip, 17
Vienna, 86–87
Vraz, Stanko, 17

Wachtel, Andrew, 17, 108
Warsaw Pact, 63
Wells, H. G., 23
Western Europe, 95–98; economic
    integration of, 99; European Union
    and, 95; illusions of, 100
Western literary market, 41
World War I, 10, 12, 67
World War II, 2, 12; Europe after, 59,
74, 96, 97

Yugoslavia, former, ix; common
    framework of, 107; communist, xi,
    38, 63, 72; cultural context of, 39–
    40; destruction of, x; federal
    parliament of, 108; immigration to,
    21; legacy of, 40; literature of, 38;
    succession of, 68. *See also* Slovenia

Zagajewski, Adam, 36
Zajc, Dane, 74
Zeitgeist, 73
Župančič, Oton, 32

About the Author

Aleš Debeljak is the director of the Center for Cultural and Religious Studies at the School of Social Sciences, University of Ljubljana, in Slovenia. He holds a doctoral degree in social theory from Syracuse University, New York. A well-respected cultural critic, he is also one of the leading poets of Central Europe and has received a number of awards, including the Slovene National Book Award, the Miriam Lindberg Israel Poetry for Peace Prize (Tel Aviv) and the Chiqyu Poetry Prize (Tokyo). His books have appeared in Japanese, German, Croatian, Serbian, Polish, Hungarian, Czech, Spanish, Slovak, Lithuanian, Finnish, Italian, and Romanian translations. Recent publications in English include *Reluctant Modernity; Twilight of the Idols: Recollections of a Lost Yugoslavia;* and three books of poetry, *Anxious Moments*, *The City and the Child,* and *Dictionary of Silence.* He has also translated a book of John Ashbery's poems into Slovene, as well as a book on the sociology of knowledge. He is general editor of the book series Terra Incognita: Writings from Central Europe, published by White Pine Press in Buffalo, New York. He and his American wife, together with their three children, make their home in Ljubljana.